THE
SPINDLE OF MEANING

By

Ronald Harvey

The

URANIA TRUST

The Urania Trust

396 Caledonian Road
London, N1 1DN.

A registered educational
charity, number 313780.

The Spindle of Meaning

By Ronald Harvey

First Edition,
Copyright © Ronald Harvey 1996.

ISBN 1 871 989 04 3

British Library Catalogue-in-Publication Data.
A catalogue record for this book is
available from the British Library.

Ronald Harvey asserts the moral right to
be identified as the author of this work.

All rights reserved. No part of this publication may be
reproduced, stored in a retrieval system, or transmitted
in any form or by any means, electronic, mechanical,
photocopying, storage or otherwise, without the prior
permission of the publishers.

Illustrations drawn by David Holmes

Typeset by T J Addey.

Printed in England by Antony Rowe, Chippenham, Wiltshire.

CONTENTS

		Introduction 3
Chapter	I	Symbols and Participation 7
	II	The Logic of the Structure 17
	III	The Structure of Meaning 21
	IV	The Elements 51
	V	Wholes, Hemispheres and Quadrants 63
	VI	The Signs of the Zodiac 69
	VII	The Geometry of Meaning 107
	VIII	Sun, Moon and Planets 121
	IX	Houses of Contention 141
	X	Temporal Change 149
	XI	Proof 155
	XII	End Piece 159
		Notes 167
		Appendix I 180
		Appendix II 184
		Glossary 187
		Bibliography 192
		Index 197

TABLE OF DIAGRAMS

1	Fields of Interest	2
2	Circles of Meaning (The Houses)	19
3	Circles of Meaning (The Zodiac)	19
4	Quaternions (1)	26
5	Quaternions (2)	27
6	Quaternions (3)	28
7	Quaternions (4)	28
8	The Role of the Houses	30
9	The Triplicities	55
10	The Quadruplicities	56
11	Parts and Wholes	64
12	The Hemispheres	65
13	Sectors and Quadrants (1)	67
14	Sectors and Quadrants (2)	67
15	The Balance of the Zodiac	73
16	Gemini and Sagittarius	82
17	The Platonic Solids	108
18	Spira Mirabilis	114
19	The Circle divided by Kepler	117
20	Extrinsic and Intrinsic Opposition	123
21	Higher Octave Planets	137
22	Albert Einstein. The Conventional Chart	142
23	" " Zodiacal Chart	143
24	" " Equal House	144
25	" " Derived Ascendant	145
26	" " Composite Ascendant	146
27	" " General Theory of Relativity	151
28	" " Thirty Degree Chart	152
29	Cusps as Centres of Houses	189

Look round our world; behold the chain of love
Combining all below and all above.
See plastic Nature working to this end,
The single atoms each to other tend,
Attract, attracted to, the next in place
Form'd and impell'd its neighbour to embrace.
See Matter next, with various life endued,
Press to one centre still, the general good.
See dying vegetables life sustain,
See life dissolving vegetate again:
All forms that perish other forms supply;
(By turns we catch the vital breath, and die)
Like bubbles on the sea of Matter borne,
They rise, they break, and to that sea return.
Nothing is foreign; parts relate to whole;
One all-extending, all-preserving soul
Connects each being, greatest with the least;
Made beast in aid of man, and man of beast;
All served, all serving: nothing stands alone:
The chain holds on, and where it ends, unknown.

Alexander Pope

'Periculosum est credere et non credere'. 'Both belief and disbelief are dangerous. Hippolitus died because his stepmother was believed. Troy fell because Cassandra was not believed. Therefore truth should be investigated long before foolish opinion can properly judge.'

Jacobus Grandamicus, 1588-1672

Figure 1 - Fields of Interest and of Potential Manifestation.

Each of the twelve sectors can be interpreted either as outer or inner experience according to context.

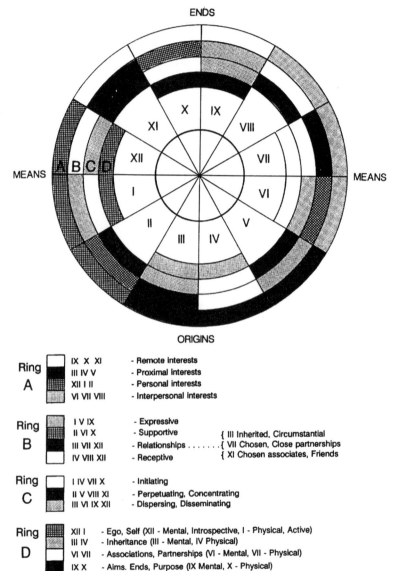

INTRODUCTION

'If someone tells me that in making these conclusions I have gone beyond the facts, I reply: "It is true that I have freely put myself among ideas which cannot rigorously be proved. That is my way of looking at things".

Pasteur.

As an eclectic reader and perpetual student of philosophy it occurred to me that what was much needed was some logical structure, a symbolism and a methodology to which varying philosophical theories could be graphically related. Some years ago, when reading Ernst Cassirer's 'Philosophy of Symbolic Forms', I was struck by his remark that those two 'Great Circles' that quarter our Earth, the Meridian and Horizon, transposed as two-dimensional diameters of a circle, formed the first basic system of co-ordinates not only for orienting us in space and time but for providing us with a structure which could be employed for discovering inter-relationships within categories of meaning. Cassirer pointed out that this basic scheme not only influenced the lay-out of cities and Roman camps but formed a framework for ideas basic to law, religion and even science. It then occurred to me that we already had such a system, providentially furnished with a relevant structure and symbolism, but that it had been ignored or ridiculed because of its illogical past and presumed irrational origin. The system was that of astrology.

My investigation of astrology was hindered by the fact that books on the subject appeared largely to be written for popular consumption and little attempt to discover an acceptable rationale behind it was evident. I was helped in discovering such a rationale by reading Dane Rudhyar's 'The Astrology of Personality'[1] but the best and by far the most comprehensive exposition I have come across is Thomas Ring's 'Astrologische Menschenkunde'[2], a monumental work in four volumes with an introduction by Professor Dr. Hans Bender of the University of Freiburg. Unfortunately, the work is not yet available in English. Another useful source was Dr. Freiherr von Klöckler's[3] 'Grundlagen für die Astrologische Deutung' and, by the same author, 'Astrologie als Erfahrungswissenschaft' with a foreword by the internationally known biologist Professor Hans Driesch. In the English language again there is, or was, a translation from the German of the philosopher Hermann Keyserling's 'Das Weltbild der Astrologie' though it is almost certainly now out of print. In retrospect much of the rationale is implicit and readily discoverable in the structure and symbolism of astrology itself, nevertheless I am deeply indebted to the above authors.

A stumbling block to some opponents of astrology has been the fact that, after Copernicus, surely everyone now knew that the earth was not the centre of the solar system and that it, disobligingly for astrology, revolved around the sun. But those who think so seem to have forgotten Einstein for, since the Theory of Relativity, it is now recognized that any point in the universe may be taken as its centre. Our experience of our world is centred on ourselves and we are creatures of the earth. In the words of Protagoras, 'man is the measure of all things'. The focal point for astrology is the individual grounded or 'earthed' at a certain point located in time by the rotation of the earth, and in space by latitude and longitude. This is also the focal point or point of origin for science and indeed all knowledge. Cassirer's structure for meaning, the Meridian and Horizon, depends on it. We are here at the crossing of these two diameters and we cannot start from anywhere else; it is from here that everything is measured.

Science since Planck and Einstein has overturned what were assumed to be its former foundations. We can no longer, God-like, stand apart from our world and examine it objectively. We now know that this is impossible; we are inextricably enmeshed in it, part of it. In this respect at least, science has been forced by its own discoveries to come to a conclusion that has formed the basis of astrology for millennia. It is now nearly a century since the Quantum Theory first surprised the world, overturned convention and revolutionised classical science, yet the man in the street has not yet fully recognized its import for science, let alone astrology. As Cassirer remarked, 'Quantum physics is in a sense the true Renaissance, the renovation and confirmation of the classical Pythagorean ideal.... Science no longer speaks the language of common sense; it speaks Pythagorean language'. This is, of course, the language of astrology, and always has been.

One of the difficulties preventing scientists from taking astrology seriously is convention. We mean here the average scientist, not the Einsteins and Niels Bohrs who were prepared to break convention and if they had not would never have made their discoveries. A favourite adjective of the scientist is 'rigorous' and rigorous means a strict, exact conformity with laws and conventions. If one keeps within the convention one is listened to but not otherwise. The testimonies of Copernicus, William Harvey, Einstein and others to the opposition they encountered to their discoveries from other scientists makes depressing reading. Radical new discovery means a breaking of convention and most scientists are conventional people. Astrology is so far outside the pale of convention that it is considered not to merit any attention at all and so, *a priori*, and without further enquiry, is condemned as nonsense.[†] No one seems to have got around to re-considering it in the light of quantum theory.

Astrology, of course, has its own conventions but they are not rigid in the sense that scientific conventions are; they are relatively vague, general and above all open-ended. Science establishes facts. Astrology suggests ideas. The logic of science is linear, from A to B to C to D to Z. The rationale of astrology is circular or, if one brings in time, spiral. The methodology of science is precise, predictable, with certainty as the aim. Experiments can be repeated and repetition presumes proof. But, as Popper remarks in 'The Logic of Scientific Discovery', 'certainty is a chimera'. 'All repetitions are *approximate repetitions*. If you insist on strict proof (or strict disproof) in the empirical sciences, you will never learn from experience, and never learn from it how wrong you are'. The unattainability of certain knowledge had, indeed, been put much earlier, in the first century B.C., by Aenesidemus the Sceptic: 'All supposed knowledge is predication. All predicates give us only the relation of things to other things or to ourselves; they never tell us what the thing itself is'. In contrast the methodology of astrology is imprecise and suggestive. Events are never exactly repeated and cannot be, which is one reason why attempts to confirm or confute astrology are not, and cannot be, conclusive. If one wants to probe astrology further one must take its methodology and symbolism on trust and listen to what it says. It will no doubt come up with more

---

[†] 'If you believe in astrology, you will attach importance to the assemblage of persons born under a certain planet; if you do not, you will regard such an assemblage as fictive. These distinctions are not logical; from a logical point of view, all assemblages of individuals are equally real or equally fictive'. (Bertrand Russell: *Human Knowledge. It's Scope and Limits.*)

questions than answers, but then, as Karl Popper remarked in another context, it is the quest that matters, seeking not finding.

To sum up, the ontology of astrology, its theory of existence, depends on the following factors in its structure and symbolism: The Horizon, where existence relates to actual, immediate, exterior experience, and The Meridian relating to mental, protracted, inner experience, these two diameters forming the basis for Cassirer's structure of meaning. But astrology goes further and puts flesh on this bare skeletal frame. It adds the Zodiacal Signs relating to potential categories of existence, and the sun, moon and planets relating as 'universals'[4] to predispositions or propensities. Its structure and symbolism suggest a scale of 'Becoming' from 'ideal' to 'real', from 'universal' to 'particular'. The more 'real' aspects of existence take their place toward the Horizon end of the scale, the more ideal or universal toward the planetary end of the scale. The structure is interrelated by geometry and logic, the symbolism by analogy and affinity. Within the planetary or 'universal' range there is yet another scale in which those bodies nearest the earth, the Moon, Sun, Mercury, Venus and Mars are taken to be more intimate or 'personal', if one can so describe a universal, whereas the outermost are deemed more remote, impersonal and archetypal, while those beyond Saturn - Uranus, Neptune and Pluto - are so far out as to be capable of accommodating the genius and the para-normal. We have, then, a wide range of meaning extending from the ideal to the real, the abstract to the concrete, the universal to the particular, and the mind to the body and, by extension the environment, and beyond that to the world. The whole structural and symbolic schema provides us with a system by which we can interpret our world and nature and discover how we are sewn into it.

I. SYMBOLS AND PARTICIPATION

Die Welt, die hält dich nicht: du selber bist die Welt,
Die dich in dir mit dir so stark gefangen hat.
(The world does not hold you: you yourself are
the world which so powerfully imprisons you).
Johannes Scheffler: *Angelus Silesius*

Our understanding of nature and of ourselves is helped by the use of symbols. Without symbols we would be hard put to it to understand anything. It has been said that the human being is as much defined by his use of symbols as by his reason ('humo sapiens') or by his use of tools ('homo faber') so that we might just as well describe him as 'homo symbolicus'.[1] Symbols are also the currency of discovery and their interpretation and manipulation by such people as Galileo, Newton and Einstein has revolutionized our view of the world.

The symbolism of astrology is abetted by analogy, by association by affinity and by association by contrast. In his Essay on the Creative Imagination Ribot writes: 'Analogy, an unstable process, undulating and multiform, gives rise to the most unforeseen and novel groupings. Through its pliability, which is almost unlimited, it produces in equal measure absurd comparisons and very original inventions.' 'Plurimum amo analogias', wrote Kepler and Galileo was an acknowledged master of analogy. Association by affinity or resemblance is self explanatory while association by contrast is according to Ribot 'full of unforeseen possibilities' and 'lends itself easily to novel relations'. The force of this remark will become evident as we examine the structure of astrology.

The symbolism of the planets beyond Saturn is capable of accommodating the unusual, the abnormal and para-normal, the extremes of experience at both ends of the spectrum, for better or worse. We have, then, a gamut of meaning, of analogy and affinity and with this in mind it is easier to recognize why Galileo, Copernicus[2], Kepler and Tycho Brahe all studied astrology. It is absurd to imagine, as some have, that it was the popular aspect of astrology that interested them. They were no doubt also influenced by Plato's 'Timaeus', arguably the first astrological book ever written, a mine of seminal ideas and a major source-book of the Renaissance. It is not impossible to accept that they found that the symbolism of astrology, embodying both reason and imagination in a systematic structure, helped them formulate their own theories. Kepler, indeed, admitted as much. Astrology is a heuristic instrument, a system for discovery.

Planetary symbols are not primarily representative of things but are, rather, vehicles for concepts. As Plato warned us when discussing the 'elements' in the Timaeus, of the element Fire, 'we should speak of it not as *being a thing* but as *having a quality*.' Symbols can be regarded as qualitative references for the mind to experience and work on. Moreover they are not to be considered alone but as integrated into a pattern, a 'Gestalt'.[3] In the horoscope the symbols interconnect and interact. The whole pattern, moving and changing with time, can be considered as forming a blue-print or template by means of which we can interpret ideas, confirm our suspicions or originate new concepts. The symbols are multi-valent and each stands for a variety of meanings, or clusters of related meanings. The horoscope never tells us which meaning is relevant in any particular case, only the *category* of meaning. It is the fact, the event itself, which selects our the relevant meaning from its category. The horoscope is a pattern, not of actuality but of potentiality.[4] It suggests to us what may potentially happen, not what will happen, not the precise event but the sort, the quality or category of event. It is vague, elastic and open-ended in contrast to the scientific approach which is precise, rigorous and deterministic. Deductively we can use the general symbol to indicate the class or category of event, but not the particular event. Inductively we can relate the particular event back to the general symbol when the relationship between particular and general, actual and potential will be found to correspond.

In spite of the often ludicrous attempts of popular astrologers to divine particular facts from general indications, astrology proper is concerned with ideas rather than facts. Even when brought down to earth by being based on the rotation and revolution of the earth at a moment in time it is nevertheless abstract. We are dealing with the realm of 'ideas', Plato's *hyperouranios topos* or super-celestial place, not the solid, palpable world of phenomena. The aim of astrology is not fortune-telling but Plato's *megiston mathema*, 'the highest knowledge or wisdom'.[5] The realm of ideas, of which astrology is a geometrical representation in time is linked to what we call reality as ideas are to facts. The events of the world are seen as participating (Plato's *methexis*) in the 'Ideas' and it is to the ideas that events or things owe their being, or conversely the Ideas are present in the things, the link between the two being situated indefinitely between 'being' and 'non-being'.

Two thousand years after Plato, Kant took up the problem of the relationship between 'real' and 'ideal' and restated it in his 'phenomenon' or thing perceived, and 'noumenon' or thing in itself ('Ding an sich'). The phenomena make up what we call our real world, the world of trees, rivers, mountains, houses and cities, but since these are only as they are by means of our sensory-motor equipment and our minds designed to appreciate them, they have no other existence than through us. According to Kant this does not mean that when we are not looking at a tree there is nothing there. There is something there, a sort of non-physical substratum, which materializes again as a tree when we look at it once more. This non-physical presence is what Kant calls the 'thing in itself', the noumenon. The thing in itself is unknowable but it must belong to some substructural or potential world interpenetrating or transcending our perceived or 'natural' world. We can say that the tree exists in potentiality and is not actualised as a tree we can touch or climb until we materialize it ourselves through our minds and sense organs.

The Platonist philosopher Alfred North Whitehead[6] describes the situation as follows: 'Thus nature gets credit which should in truth be reserved for ourselves; the rose for its scent, the nightingale for his song, and the sun for his radiance. The poets are entirely mistaken. They should address their lyrics to themselves and should turn into odes of self-congratulation on the excellency of the human mind'.

Kant's conclusion was later disputed by Hegel who asked himself - why assume that there is a thing-in-itself at all? Even according to Kantian reasoning it was self-contradictory; why not suppose that there is no thing-in-itself and that appearances are all. Nature as it appears to us was, after all, not an illusion. It was real, even though its existence depended on our experience of it. Like the famous Zen Buddhist saying: 'Before you study Zen, mountains are mountains and rivers are rivers; while you are studying Zen, mountains are no longer mountains and rivers are no longer rivers; but once you have had enlightenment, mountains are once again mountains and rivers again rivers'.

With the thing-in-itself out of the way we are left with the real world constructed by ourselves. This bewildering conclusion appears to be increasingly confirmed the further scientists probe into modern quantum physics. This phenomenological aspect of Hegel's philosophy fits in well with the structure and significance of astrology, as does his 'dialectic', of which more later. Professor Michael Whiteman claims that the gap between one observation of the tree and another observation of the same is bridged by a potential so that we can say that the tree exists in potentiality and is not actualized except when someone observes it. This idea of a potential world is one that we shall use in our enquiry into astrology. In other words our world is fashioned out of our experience, our participation (methexis). As our world creates us so we create our world. We are in an unavoidable 'double-bind' with it all. This view is reminiscent of Jung's ideas of the 'Unus Mundus' which he applied to one aspect of the unity of existence and which became only sporadically actualized in inner and outer experience. In Jung's view the Unus Mundus contained all the preconditions necessary for the formation of actual phenomena. The phenomenological philosopher Husserl claims that the essence of objects is correlative with states of mind and that no distinction can be made between what is perceived and the actual perception itself. Experience, participation, goes further than sense perception and embraces whatever the mind conceives, e.g., the inner world of feeling, emotions or abstract thought. This is perhaps as near as one can get to what astrology is largely about.

The horoscope then is not a map of actuality but of potentiality.† It is a chart of Ideas or Forms which may, or may not, be realized in actual events at any particular time. It assumes that behind the world of experience lies a latent, potential world, a world of possibilities capable of realization in a myriad different forms. The Ideas like the symbols representing them are 'universals'; their realizations, the events to which they point but do not cause, are 'particulars'. Between the 'ideal' and the 'real' stretches the potential embracing categories of related meaning, each category depending from its source Idea, the universal.

---

† 'Der Mensch....muss sich selbst zu dem machen, was er sein soll'. (Man must make himself what he ought to be). 'Was er unmittelbar ist, ist nur die Möglichkeit, es zu sein'. (What he is directly, is only the possibility of becoming so). (Hegel: 'Philosophie der Weltgeschichte').

Deduction	Ideas (Universals)	
↓	Categories	
	Space-Time	↑
	Phenomena (Particulars)	Induction

Perhaps it should be explained what is meant by universals and particulars in astrology. Universals are abstract principles broadly corresponding to Plato's 'Ideas' or 'Forms' and symbolized by the heavenly bodies - Mars, Venus and so on. Particulars are the events or concrete objects, i.e., actual examples of the general abstract principles suggested by the universal symbols. Universals are general, vague and inclusive; particulars are individual, precise and exclusive of other particulars. Between the general and the particular we have categories and sub-categories of meaning in descending scale from ideal to real.[†] The symbol Saturn, for instance, as universal subtends a number of categories, e.g., hardness, rigidity, gravity, authority, convention, tradition, seriousness, weight, frustration, pessimism, caution, restriction and so on. As particular it may relate to a restrictive event, a fall, a particular hardness, e.g., a bone, a stone, a lump of lead which is not only hard but heavy also. The universal itself cannot be described except in such vague terms as Saturn-like, Mars-like, Venus-like and so on.

Each universal symbol has general meaning in terms of relationship, not of substance. For substance we have to go further down the scale to particulars. The symbol forms the nucleus of a 'family' - a meaningful family. We cannot say just what it is that relates one member of the family to another, or to the parent symbol, but we can immediately recognize the family likeness. The relationship or resemblance is in part logical, in part etymological and in part archetypal. Each symbol is also a focus for both analogy and affinity. Affinity could be described as an a-causal principle linking like with like in a kind of selective resonance. It was a feature of Pythagorean thinking, of Hippocrates' 'sympathy of all things', and

---

[†] In Plato if the Idea or Form (the Universal) is regarded as an exemplar then phenomena either partake in it (methexis) or imitate it (mimēsis). In astrology for instance a particular stone partakes in or copies the qualities of its universal (Saturn) while the universal in turn partakes in the actual materialisation, in a quality such as hardness, heaviness, impenetrability and so on.

runs through the teachings of Taoism, the Neo-Platonists and thinkers of the Renaissance such as Bruno and Pico della Mirandola.

Suppose we take the moon as an example.[7] In astrology as in countless mythologies the moon has been a feminine and maternal symbol. The lunar family and its nature are illustrated by a complex of related ideas and the words used to describe them. Take, for instance, the word 'mother'. This comes from Latin 'mater', Greek 'meter' and Sanskrit 'matar', but the root of the word is 'ma' meaning breast (of. mamma, mammary, mammal). Cognate with the Latin 'mater' is the word 'matrix' meaning womb, for which the Greek word was 'metra'. The fundamental meaning of the word mother is, then, breast or womb and all that they imply from conception and birth to care and nourishment. The Greek word for moon is 'mene' and the word for month 'men' (Lat. 'mensis') from which we get the words 'mensual' and 'menstruation'. It is in this light that planetary symbols have to be understood. Each symbol is a focus for a network of relationships which, though they may at first appear to have little in common, yet can be recognized as being part of a family.[8] And when we know the type of family relations of each symbol we are in a position to assign any particular idea to its appropriate symbol.

To return once more to the realization of potentials, if a particular event is not realized all we have is the idea or form, the promise unfulfilled, the embryo still-born, latent in the 'womb of becoming', e.g., Plato's 'Receptacle', which latter A.N. Whitehead likens to space or space-time. The potential links the universal above with the particular below. In a sense universal and particular are mutual participants. To Goethe the particular and universal interpenetrated each other. There is also an interplay between potential and actual, a mutual participation with the species coming as intermediary. Thomas Aquinas said much the same: 'Anima enim quasi transformata est in rem per speciem' (De Natura Verbi Intellectus). It is one of the limitations of astrology, as it is of life, that potentialities are not always, indeed one might say seldom, realized.

If astrology owes a great deal to Plato it owes much, too, to Aristotle. The idea of 'potentia' (Gk. 'dynamis') underlies the potentiality latent not only in Hegel and Husserl but in astrology itself. In Aristotle that which brings about the materialisation of universals is 'entelechy' with which is associated the sister idea of 'teleology'. The importance of these two ideas for astrology is that entelechy is 'inner design', teleology 'external design'. Both Aristotle and Hegel insist that life is a process of design and it is difficult in examining astrology to avoid the thought that without design it would have no raison d'être.† With entelechy the ends and aims of an organism are contained within it. With teleology the ends are outside it. If one considers the problem - Which came first, the chicken or the egg? - then, from the entelechy point of view the egg came first, its aim being to become a chicken, the end is within itself. From the teleological point of view, however, the chicken came first; its aim is to produce an egg. The end is outside itself.

According to Aristotle organisms change because of the potentialities inherent in them, the aim being to attain their perfection. Unlike Plato the Ideas or Forms are *in* the organism not outside it. Evolution proceeds not by material causes 'pushing from behind', but by final causes 'pulling from in front'. Everything is directed toward an end which is potentially inside it as final cause. Essentially final cause and formal cause are the same. Both Hegel and the biologist Woodger describe entelechy as 'internal teleology' or 'inner design'. The entelechy of an acorn is an oak, that of a child the summit of achievement or individuation, the mature adult. The entelechy is formative following certain paths of development to which the biologist, the late C.H. Waddington, gave the name 'chreodes'. Formative forces have had a long history including Galen's 'dynamis diaplastike', Kepler's 'facultas formatrix' and Goethe's 'Urpflanze'. Kepler's theory is especially noteworthy here as it relates to astrology.[9]

In contrast to entelechy, teleology has its end or purpose outside itself. An example is the state or the welfare of others regarded as an end for individuals, e.g., Hegel's philosophy of history. Politically teleology may lead to the idealisation of the group, the tribe or nation, or on the other hand to altruism of some sort, socialism,

---

† Allport claims that the activity of a person is purposive.... 'every state of the person is pointed in the direction of future possibilities' and he compares this with Aristotle's doctrines of 'orexis' (longing, yearning) and 'entelechy' (complete actualization of a thing)....'the human infant will in time.... become some sort of structural system, self-regulating and self-maintaining.... he will exert himself to become something more than a stencil copy of the species to which he belongs'. Such capacities, he says, are not instincts but 'are of the sort to ensure growth and orderly structure.' (Gordon Allport: *Becoming - Basic Considerations for a Psychology of Personality*. Yale University Press, 1955).

communism or group 'ism'. The community of nations, the United Nations, is an example of teleology, as is also concern for the environment. The influence of teleological ideas can be seen in the writings of Giambattista Vico (Principi della Scienza Nuova, 1725) and the theoretical histories of Hegel, Marx, Spengler and Arnold Toynbee. While they differ in many respects they all agree that the historical process is not accidental but follows certain principles.

Entelechy or 'inner design', however, fosters self-improvement and personal achievement within the individual, emphasizing, in contrast to teleology, the importance of heredity. Unfortunately the perversity of human nature is such that what is inner design gets imposed on the outer world and what is outer design is sometimes operative within the individual so that personal achievement (inner) is often at the expense of others (outer), heredity (inner) results in class distinction (outer) while egalitarianism (outer) becomes mediocrity (inner). The inner aim is *arete*, personal excellence, the outer aim, fraternity and altruism, but when transposed they present a gruesome picture of the Right and Left in political parties.

In biology the idea of purpose has had a bad press, being anathema to mechanistic dogma, in spite of the efforts of vitalists like Hans Driesch and ideas associated with Henri Bergson's 'élan vital'. Now, however, things seem to be beginning to change with new theories of biological development with a definite teleological element coming to the fore, where previously it had been kept in what was thought decent obscurity.† As one scientist put it: Teleology is a lady without whom no biologist can live; yet he is ashamed to show himself in public with her'.

Teleology, or rather entelechy, was recognized by Goethe. In his poem 'Metamorphose der Tiere' (Metamorphosis of Animals) he writes: 'Zweck sein selbst ist jegliches Tier.....Alle Glieder bilden sich nach ewgen Gesetzen...' (Every animal is an end in itself.... all limbs develop according to eternal laws). Entelechy involves regular change, the blue-print for such change providing the 'facultas formatrix' shaping us towards our ends. In the process cells die and are rejected while others take their place. After a time, usually given

---

† Biological thinkers supporting some form of teleological process or 'purpose' include Oparin, Sherrington, Lillie, Agar, E.S. Russell, E.W. Sinnot, von Bertalanffy and C.H. Waddington. (see Errol Harris: 'The Foundations of Metaphysics in Science', Allen and Unwin, p. 61).

as about seven years, our bodies have changed completely. There is not a single cell in the whole body which has not been replaced (except brain cells). Nothing of us is as it was. The eyes, the nose, the skin that marked us out before are now no more. In Plato's 'Symposium' Diotima says to Socrates; 'Even during the period for which any living being is said to live and retain his identity - as a man, for example, is called the same from boyhood to old age - he does not in fact retain the same attributes, although he is called the same person; he is always becoming a new being and undergoing a process of loss and reparation, which effects his hair, his flesh, his bones, his blood, and his whole body'. Such entelechy, or purposeful development, is represented in astrology, as we shall see later, in the development of the horoscope in time.

As we have remarked, in Aristotelian theory organisms change because of the potentialities inherent in them.† In astrology categorical meanings of universals such as Mercury, Venus or Mars are to some extent hierarchical suggesting a scale of existence from ideal to real corresponding with Aristotle's *potentiality* and *actuality*. An actual event, person or thing arising out of its potential to become an event, person or thing, e.g., an end or aim for that particular potentiality, may in turn become a potential for a further aim or end. Let us look at Mars. In the list of potential meanings depending from the universal we have the word anger, anger in potential. If anger should materialize it in turn becomes a potential for an actual quarrel although it may not materialize as such. If it does develop into an actual quarrel this in turn may become a potential for a fight, and so we may continue from potential to actual with meanings encapsulated in a series of chinese boxes, one within the other. Take now the universal, the Moon, one of whose potential meanings is mother. Suppose the potential materialized into an actual mother. A mother has potentiality for pregnancy. The potentiality materializes in an actual pregnancy. Pregnancy in turn is potential for the birth of a child. The potential, the foetus, may miscarry and the child never reach actuality. But if it does and it is a boy the ensuing list of potentialities goes off in one direction; if a girl in another. A girl is again a potentiality for a mother. She

---

† 'An organic product of nature is an individual in which everything is alternately purpose and means. Nothing in it is fortuitous, nothing is without purpose.' (Karl Jaspers).

may never become one; she may die in childhood or perhaps be infertile. But if she achieves actual motherhood then the round of potentiality-actuality-potentiality, mother-child-mother may continue. Origins turn into ends and ends into origins. Potentia becomes Actus and Actus Potentia. When we observe that an actual event in real life corresponds with its potential symbol in the horoscope we have to recognize that it too may be a potential for something further. Within its category of meaning potentiality has no limits. It can go on till the crack of doom. Actuality on the other hand is limited to the space-time perimeter and character of the event. Only as further potential can actuality achieve a life beyond the instantaneous grave. This Aristotelian view-point is, of course, only one among others, but it may help to throw light on the progression from universal to particular, from ideal to real.

II. THE LOGIC OF THE STRUCTURE

We must now look more closely at Cassirer's schematic framework for meaning - the crossing of the two diameters, the Meridian and Horizon which the Romans used for orienting their Decumanus and Cardo, the two main thoroughfares quartering their military camps and cities. It would appear that the Meridian-Horizon structure is somehow deeply rooted in the human psyche. This is reinforced when we recognise that the structure together with the twelve sectors of the circle depending from it is grounded in number, not so much number *per se* but in the Pythagorean sense of qualitative number in which number is linked to meaning.[1] The numbers three, four and twelve underlie the basic structure as they do in astrology. There are three sets of four 'elements' and four sets of three qualities, making up the twelve signs of the zodiac. Kant was no astrologer but it is perhaps worth noting that in The Critique of Pure Reason he established twelve *a priori* categories of meaning, the twelve being again divided into threes and fours. Instances of this 3 - 4 - 12 division are legion.[2] In Aristotle's logic a syllogism has three propositions and there are four kinds of syllogism, moreover there are sixty-four (four to the power of three) possible form combinations. The mediaeval university or 'studium generale' divided its faculties into the 'Trivium' and 'Quadrivium'. This three-four division now appears to be cropping up in genetics. The genetic code DNA consists of four bases, Adenine, Thymine, Guanine and Cytosine. From these four bases, again as in Aristotle, four to the power of three, sixty-four different nucleotide triplets arise, moreover the messenger code RNA also uses triplets to form its basic figure. In the Chinese 'I Ching' or book of changes each hexagram is made up of two basic trigrams, i.e., a three line figure. Here again four to the power of three produces the sixty-four hexagrams of meaning which make up the I Ching. Number, according to Jung, regulates both psyche and matter and von Franz suggests that 'quaternary numbers' are connected with the process of becoming conscious or with wholeness, while 'triadic numbers' are related to intellectual and physical movement. Quaternary instances are the four dimensions of the space-time continuum, the four forces of nature (nuclear, electro-magnetic, weak (beta decay) and gravity), Schopenhauer's four-fold root of the Principle of Sufficient Reason, Jung's four 'psychic functions' and, in embryology, the four-fold structure of the morula after the male gamete has met the female oozyte. Other fours come to mind, as also threes. Number, according to von Franz, is a common ordering factor bringing both psyche and matter together, structuring both. We suggest, following Cassirer, that geometrical structure is equally important.

The three-four-twelve structure of the horoscope can, of course, be looked at in various ways. One could, perhaps, regard the twelve poles of the six diameters as divided space into a sort of map or spatial organisation on which we may plot whatever we want provided its intrinsic coherence fits the logic of the situation. In astrology we cannot do this for each pole is already saddled *a priori* with a nexus of meaning derived from its geometry, a geometry based on the rotation of the earth in space externally and on the structure of the psyche internally. The two main axes of this structure orient us in space and time, the Meridian relating to time, the Horizon to space or place, direction and orientation.

In his 'Critique of Pure Reason' Kant regarded space as relating to exterior sense, time to interior sense. In other words the Meridian relates to inner experience, i.e., the mind, while the Horizon concerns outer experience obtained through the body and sense data, and by extension, the environment. This accords with the symbolism inherent in the structure of astrology. If we now take the idea of teleology and seek a place for it on one of these diameters we can see that since it is based on time, and on purpose which is mind directed, it must logically be accommodated on the Meridian. At the lower pole of the Meridian, the Lower Heaven, we have ARCHE (origins), at the upper pole, the Midheaven, we have TELOS (ends),[3] while on the Horizon we have means, the Ascendant pole representing VOLUNTAS (will) and the Descendant ARBITRIUM (choice), the Horizon being the axis of free-will, the Meridian that of necessity. Teleology being end-seeking originates at Arche and is drawn to its completion at Telos. The acorn at the foot, activated by the particular entelechy coiled up inside it, affected externally by the means - soil, water and air which together with sunlight enable carbon dioxide exchange to take place essential to its growth - and pulled up by the general purpose of all acorns to become oaks, strives to realize its aim. Note the part placed by the four elements Earth, Water, Air and Fire (sunlight). The Meridian, however, can be read in two ways - as a causal development in time, or as a logical, a temporal relation between premise and consequence. Causally the Arche always precedes the Telos, i.e., the first cause precedes the final cause. A-temporally, however, the final cause can become the premise from which follow logical consequences, so that the 'flow' of meaning is reversed. This is most evident in the interplay between opposing signs of the zodiac.

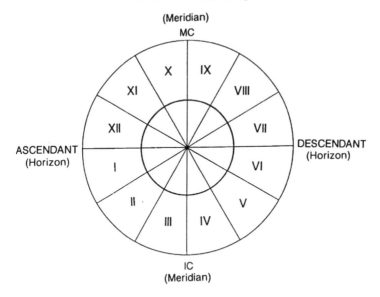

Figure 2 The Horoscope of Fields of Interest and Potential Manifestation.

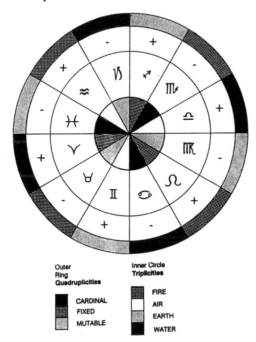

Figure 3 The Zodiac as Fields of Physical & Mental, Exernal & Internal Potentiality.

The Meridian and Horizon as axes of meaning may also provide us with an interesting supposition concerning morality, an unorthodox departure since generally speaking ethics is beyond the compass of the structure and symbolism of astrology, which is ethically neutral. We will take the contrasting claims of hierarchy and egalitarianism. Hierarchy which relates to the Meridian could be described as a vertical quality, egalitarianism a horizontal one. The inference is that hierarchy is not for society (Horizon); it is for the individual. It embraces ideas of better or worse, higher and lower, an internal ladder if you like. Egalitarianism is external, for society, for relationships with others. It carries with it ideas of equality, fairness, justice, sharing, participating and so on. It is a social quality. The trouble comes when each quality operates in the wrong field. Egalitarianism in the internal field leads to mediocrity, vacillation and loss of decision - one thing is as good as another. Hierarchy in the external, social field invites domination and submission, oppression, excess opulence and penury, class distinction and class war. Hierarchy is an individual virtue but a social vice. Egalitarianism is an individual vice but a social virtue. It must be regretfully recognized that down the centuries and across the world for most of the time and in most places each quality has been operating in the wrong field. Generally speaking it has been only in the individual conscience and in such institutions as monasteries, religious, idealist of humanism communities or in those few areas of the world untouched by 'civilization', that the qualities have found their rightful place.

III. THE STRUCTURE OF MEANING

We can conceive an idea before we can find words to describe our concept. When we do find words reason is brought into play, a framework of meaning is constructed within which our concept is contained. The framework, built of the common instrument of understanding, language, can now be understood by others; it is now communicable whereas the pure concept was not. The fluidity of our concept is now strait-jacketed but rendered manipulable in terms of the framework and understandable in so far as the framework approximates to it and does not unduly distort it.

The framework of meaning, which we have already touched on and are now considering further, consists primarily of the cardinal axes of the horoscope, the Meridian and Horizon, and secondarily of the twelve sectors of the circle depending from them. We can use the poles of these diameters as pegs for ideas and so long as the ideas are of the same order and one the same level we can relate them to each other in a meaningful way. Further we can watch their progression in terms of temporal and spatial relationship as the axes rotate in time. In this way they may come to variable associations with factors in the horoscope and in turn break off connections with other factors. We have a rotating geometrical figure geared to time in which relationships of different kinds are constantly being made and broken as indeed they are in life.

In mythology and in Plato's 'Republic' the Meridian was represented by the 'Spindle of Necessity'. It was the axle of the hub of the cosmos and was kept spinning by the Three Fates, Atropos, Clotho and Lachesis - Atropos singing of things to come, Clotho of the present and Lachesis of the past. In astrology it still bears the idea of necessity in contrast to the Horizon which is the axis of free-will.[1] We will deal with the Meridian first. As a vertical diameter its upper or south pole is the Midheaven (Gk. Mesouranema, Lat. Medium Coeli or MC) while its lower or north pole is the Lower Heaven (Gk. Hypopgeion, Lat. Imum Coeli or IC). The arrow of time runs up from IC to MC, from past to future, from Lachesis to Atropos. It is cut at the half way mark where sits Clotho astride the present, on the Horizon. A brief table of Meridian meaning may be helpful:

MERIDIAN
Necessity
The Mind
Succession in Time
(Le temps est le moyen offert à tout ce qui sera,
d'être afin de n'être plus. Paul Claudel.)[2]
Hierarchical relationships
Relationships in time on a basis of inequality
(e.g., parent-child)
Heredity

Midheaven
Future. Forward
Aims. Ends. Fruits.
Ambition. Purpose.
Summit. Goal.
Career.
Posterity.
Expectation. Aspiration.
Parental authority (subject as parent).
Parent as role model.
Final cause.
TELOS

Lower Heaven
Past. Backward.
Origins. Beginnings. Roots.
Instinct. Unconscious drives.
Base. Home
Inheritance.
Heredity.
Memory. Reflection.
Parental Authority (subject as child).
Parental care. Upbringing.
First cause.
ARCHE

The Meridian provides our axis for relationships in series, in succession in time, or in depth, the Horizon for those that are coeval, parallel, immediate and in breadth. While the Meridian represents succession in time at a certain place, the Horizon stands for extension in space at a certain time. The Meridian is our axis for function, the Horizon for structure. Since function and structure like energy and matter and time and space form a continuum the two axes should always be considered in relation to each other for essentially they are two aspects of the same whole. Structure can be seen as slowed down, congealed function while function can be seen as accelerated, rarefied structure. At another level of meaning the Meridian represents the idea of 'Being' rather than that of 'Becoming', the continuing identity which persists throughout ever-changing circumstances. It contains the sense of 'I'-ness that remains with us from cradle to grave, the sense that however much we have changed we are still essentially the same. A feature of the Lower Heaven is that it may stand for inherited memory, archetypal or otherwise, individual or collective, transmitting a vague, inarticulate efficaciousness of the past (of. Jung's 'vererbte Erinnerungsbilder' - inherited memory images).

The horizontal diameter of the circle, the Horizon, represents the space axis, its left-hand or eastern pole being the Ascendant (Gk. Anatole Heliou or sunrise) while the right-hand or western pole is the Descendant (Gk. Dysis Heliou or sunset). The importance of the Horizon in astrology is largely due to its role as the focus for what Whitehead[†] has called 'presentational immediacy'. It is in this present moment that the fluid potentiality of the world may become for the moment congealed in material reality. Here time and space, energy and matter, function and structure, together with our mental and physical equipment designed to apprehend them, conspire together to present us with a certain appearance which we take to be real, and indeed is real because we make it so. The Ascendant is coloured by the sign of the zodiac in which it falls so that we have, in the words of Zola in another context, 'un coin de la nature à travers un tempérament'.

The meaning of the Horizon, like those of the Meridian, are on different levels.[3] There would, for instance, appear to be little connection between free-will, structure and immediacy, but the Horizon and Meridian are universals for which depend categories of meaning at different levels of understanding. A proper appreciation of the universal will reveal that there are relationships linking such meanings somewhere in the scale between category and universal but they require a little working out.

[†] In Whitehead's view 'real' time is the duration of an actual occasion and 'real' space the extension of that occasion. Each event or occasion carries its space-time with it as part of itself. Space-time is, in effect, brought to birth by the event. Of itself, space-time does not exist. It remains 'ideal' or 'potential' until actualized by an event. This view appears to be conformable with the significance and structure of the Meridian-Horizon diameters in astrology. The Meridian and Horizon do not actually exist in the world. We construct them for our convenience and make use of them as events become actualized, and situated in time and space by them.

HORIZON[4]
Free-will
Spatial extension. Structure
The body[5]
The environment
Time contracted to the present moment.[6] Immediacy.
Relationships on a basis of equality
(e.g., Husband - wife, etc.).

Ascendant	Descendant
Subjectivity	Objectivity
The Ego. The Persona	Alter-Ego, 'Not-Self'. Other.
The person one feels oneself to be	The person one lacks and needs as complement. Husband. Wife. The
Personality	Partner. The person opposed to one. Enemy. Rival
Self-sufficiency	Interdependence
Egocentricity. 'Me first'	Altruism. 'Others too'
Single	Double or plural
Inequality	Equality
Natural impulse	Deliberation. Consideration
Exploitation of environment	Respect for environment
The world we dominate or to which we succumb	The world to which we adjust and make the best of
Action for self regardless of others	Action in co-operation, or mindful of others (Peace), or in opposition (War).
VOLUNTAS	ARBITRIUM

Since the past ('no longer') and the future ('not yet') do not exist in themselves but only in the present as memory or anticipation and purpose, the axis of immediacy, or the present moment, is the only focus for the actualization of events and the Ascendant is considered the most important point in the horoscope. There is no choice in the past, which is determined, and none in the future which we ourselves help to determine, but the present, within the constraints of a determined past and an anticipated future allows a modicum of free-will. For the moment Voluntas and Arbitrium overcome Telos and Arche and since the present is always with us, and past or future never, we have an ever-present field for choice, a field well exploited by existentialism.

We have dealt with the four cardinal radii of the circle and now we have to consider the other spokes of the wheel of becoming and the twelve sectors of the circle defined by them. These sectors are known as 'houses' (the Greeks called them 'Topoi' or 'places') which correspond analogously with the signs of the zodiac as the more particular to the more general, the more contingent and actual to the more latent and potential. The first house relates to the first sign Aries, the second to the second sign Taurus, and so on round the circle. The 'universal' meanings pertaining to the sun, moon and planets are qualified by their position in the signs and further qualified by their position in the houses so that we have two progressive stages in the scale of increasing particularisation. Since the signs and the houses rarely coincide, except spatially at the equator (0° latitude) and temporally twice in twenty-four hours at other latitudes when the Midheaven reaches 0° Cancer or 0° Capricorn, the range of meaning is considerably increased. Further particularisation is brought about by the position of the Meridian and Horizon, the Midheaven and especially the Ascendant indicating the potential event (symbolized by planet and sign) most likely for actualization.† Even at this stage it is still only potential, though if it does materialize it will bear the stamp of the symbol and sign indicated.

† Dependent Categories of Meaning

Sun, Moon and Planets   (Universals)
↓
Zodiac   (Submerged Potentials)
↓
Horoscope   (Rising Potentials)
↓
Meridian   (Surfacing Potentials)
↓
Horizon   (Surfacing Potentials)
↓
Possible materialization in Actuality.

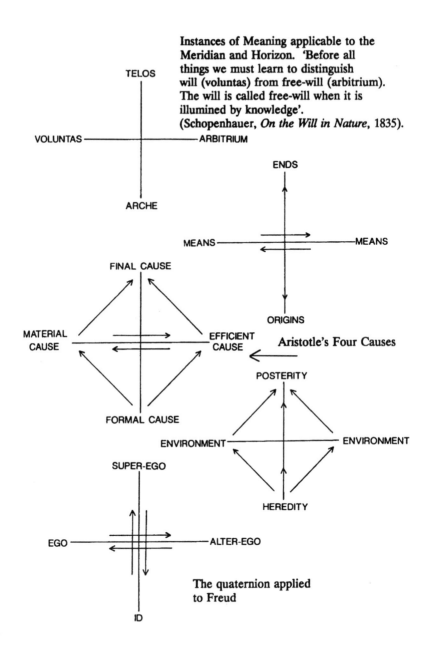

Figure 4

Each house is reflected in its opposite so that the 'harmony in contrariety' of Heraclitus and the logical 'thesis and antithesis' of Hegel are preserved, as also the causal sequence we have seen in regard to the Meridian. The logical interchange and interdependence is most evident in those houses adjoining the Horizon, the causal sequence in those adjoining the Meridian. Each house is also affected adversely by those at right angles to it, the right angle denoting a radical difference or disaffinity. Again, each house is in harmony with those at 120° from it and to a lesser degree with those at 60° from it. Finally each house begets and is, in turn, influenced by, the house which follows it, the angles 30°, 60°, 90°, 120° and 180° determining meaning and being indicative of strength of influence. The strongest aspects or angles are 180° and 90° since they relate to the geometry of the Meridian and Horizon. The next in strength are 120° and 60°, with 30° being the weakest, the greater angle in each case indicating the greater strength.

We have here, then, a coherent system and structure of meaning based on actual phenomena, the rotation and revolution of the earth, and on geometrical angle. Our horoscope is a diagram of our interrelation with the universe, our participation in it and its mutual participation in us. We are, as it were, sewn into our world and the horoscope illustrates the stitching. It represents the potential behind the peculiar symbiotic union between us and our phenomenal world. It is a herald of our participation in the design.

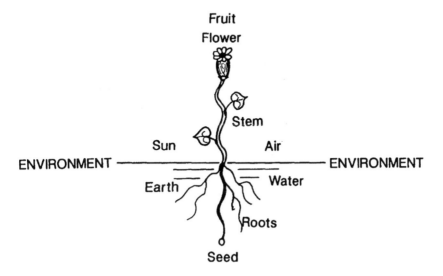

Figure 5

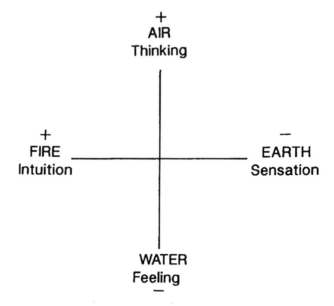

Figure 6

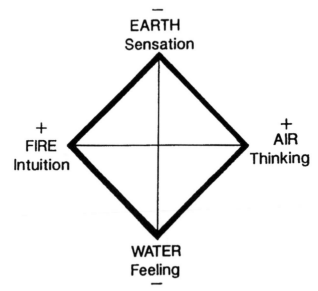

Figure 7

FIGURES 6 and 7 - JUNG'S FOUR FUNCTIONS

As usually reproduced (Fig. 6) this quaternion does not fit into the horoscope as in the latter the opposition joins signs of the same polarity whereas here it links signs of opposite polarity. To fit the horoscope it would have to be arranged as in the next diagram (Fig. 7). This demonstrates graphically the irreconcilability of opposing functions. It is here not an opposition which carries within it a synthesis as in the normal chart but a square which implies a radical difference with no possible resolution of opposites. This exactly reflects Jung's meaning. There is no redeeming feature such as similar polarity inviting the possible harmony in contrariety as in a normal opposition. Not only are the elements contrasted but the polarities too.

FIGURE 8 - THE ROLE OF THE HOUSES (Overleaf)

The houses of the horoscope indicate the direction in which the potential symbolized by signs and planets may become actualized. By actualization is meant (1) externally - manifested in action and sensation, and (2) internally - brought into consciousness. Each individual house represents a sphere of physical action or sensation, or mental interest, activity or reaction.

In angular houses the suggestion is that potentiality may manifest in activity. In succedent houses potentiality may actualize in resistance, while in cadent houses potentiality will tend to manifest in mental work or restless movement. The activity, resistance or movement will be coloured by the sign which happens to coincide with the house at the time of birth, and again at the moment of manifestation, if indeed the potentiality is in fact actualized.

The Spindle of Meaning

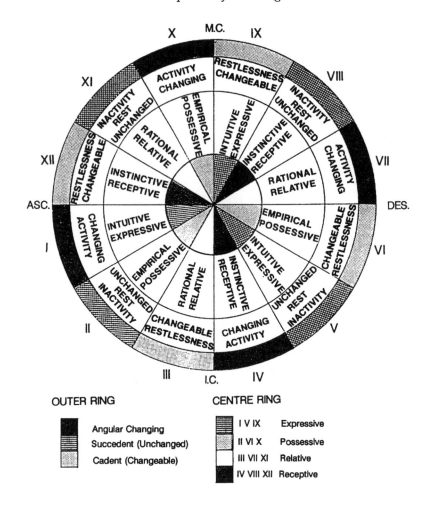

The houses, as we have said, relate to the signs, the first house to the first sign and so on, anti-clockwise round the circle. They are tabled below as in opposition, the first house confronting the seventh, its opposite and complement.

THE FIRST HOUSE   Associated sign - Aries

The focus, or 'cusp', if formed by the Ascendant (Gk., Horoskopos, i.e., 'hour indicator'). The Ascendant, and to a lesser degree the whole of the first house, stands for the focus of immediacy - the here and now - from the stand-point of self-interest, self-sufficiency and subjectivity. It represents the 'persona'. It stands for the ego as brought out by interaction with others or with the environment. It relates to Sartre's 'être pour soi' as opposed to the 'être pour autrui' of the Descendant. The interior ego or 'self' based on self-worth, ambition and purpose relates to the Midheaven. The person as he appears to others. His opinion of himself vis-a-vis others. His attitude to him immediate milieu with a view to exploiting it to this advantage regardless of others or to experiencing it in isolation. His personal *Weltanschauung*. Personal interests. Impulse. The way in which he instinctively tackles an immediate task. Self assertion. The immediate urge to do things, to make one's way in the world. Here he disturbs his environment or his fellows to suit his purpose regardless of opposition. The Ascendant is also an indicator of physical constitution and cast of mind. Its influence can often be traced, coloured by the sign in which it falls, in the type of physical build and facial characteristics, as well as in the mental 'set' of the person concerned. It is the most 'particular' and commonly the most recognizable factor in the whole horoscope, usually much more noticeable than the Sun-sign descriptions of popular astrology. It is not so well known because it depends on the time of birth as well as the day and that is not always available.

The first house is associated indirectly with the planet Mars since it is analogous to the sign Aries. More particularly it is linked with the planet associated with the zodiacal sign appearing on the Ascendant. Thus if the Ascendant is in Gemini then Mercury is considered the 'ruler' of the house and since the Ascendant is the most important point in the horoscope its associated planet is often considered the ruler of the whole horoscope. It may then play a large part in the psycho-physical constitution of the subject, moreover the sign in which it is placed qualifies the subject still further. Any planets happening to fall within the first house will also serve to emphasize the qualities of the house and in addition add their own individual significance to it. The latter sentence applies to any house, not just the first.

Each house, like each sign, is complemented by its opposite across the circle so that the meaning of one is opposed, reciprocated and reflected by the meaning of the other. In astrology one proceeds from the one to its opposite the two, then to the three and four, and finally to the twelve. The opposite of the first house is the seventh.

THE SEVENTH HOUSE[7] — Associated sign - Libra

> Nothing in the world is single,
> All things by a law divine,
> In one another's being mingle -
> Why not I with thine? *Shelley.*

The cusp is formed by the Descendant and opposes and complements the first house. This also indicates a focus on the present moment but from the standpoint of association with others or of regard for them, a relationship of reciprocity, of balance between the demands of self (first house) and the demands of others and of adjustment to environment rather than exploitation of it. It is a house of consideration rather than of impulse. In the first house one acts before one thinks. In the seventh one thinks before one acts. Here the individual attempts to right the balance disturbed in the first house, to reciprocate, or to accommodate himself to others in some sort of harmony. It is the house of the 'non-ego' or 'alter-ego'. Interdependence. While the first house stands for challenge, here the challenge is taken up and joined. The first house suggests inequality, a disturbance of equilibrium; one seeks an advantage, tries to override; the seventh stands for restoration of balance, parity, one meets others on equal terms. In contrast to the singularity of the first house the seventh exhibits a double or mirror nature. Here everything is seen in terms of balance, equality, reciprocity, conflict, compromise and co-operation, opposition and give and take. It is associated indirectly with the planet Venus and the ruler of Libra and serves as a feminine complement to the predominantly masculine aspects of the first house. All kinds of association on terms of equality, reciprocity, concord and discord are illustrated here. Partners, wives, husbands, rivals and enemies all find their place here.

It is popularly known as the 'house of marriage' and stands for the relationship with one's half or 'opposite number'. It is considered to show, from the associated sign or planet, or from any planet contained in the house, the type of complement to one's personality one seeks or needs, e.g., the type of wife or husband, business partner or associate best fitted to achieve a balanced whole. It is also known as the 'house of war' for the reciprocity is not always peaceful.[†] The opposition between seventh and first reminds one of Empedocles' 'Love and Strife' by which the world was brought into being.

The ambivalence of this house is shown in that it is also taken to denote the type of rival, opponent or enemy most likely to offer resistance to one's immediate personal activities.[‡] It is in this house that one must look for clues concerning unions, contracts, agreements, disputes, law suits, divorces, rupture of association and breaking of contract. It should be emphasized that the house does not represent the actual quality of the 'other' but only as it appears to the individual himself. The wife, husband or partner will see the relationship in a different light the quality of which should be indicated in their respective horoscopes in the same house.

[†] According to C.K. Ogden opposition involves the 'reciprocal neutralization of like actions'. Two actions which are different do not create opposition (e.g. signs in square to each other and of different polarity). In opposition the two sides must be equivalent (in astrology, of the same polarity). Difference, however great, does not involve opposition which is necessarily allied to similarity. Difference is disaffinity, alienation (the square aspect). Similarity involves both acceptance and rejection, co-operation and conflict, thesis and antithesis of equivalent terms with the possible resolution in the third term - synthesis. (C.K. Ogden: 'Opposition - A Linguistic and Psychological Analysis', Kegan Paul, 1932. See also Tarde's 'L'Opposition Universelle'.)

[‡] 'Opposition is not to be defined as the maximum degree of difference, but as a very special kind of repetition, namely of two similar things that are mutually destructive in virtue of their very similarity.... All oppositions whether in series, degrees, or signs, may take place between terms that find expression in one and the same being or in two different beings.... It is internal oppositions (in the same being) which make external oppositions (between different beings) possible'. (C.K. Ogden).

These two Horizon-based houses illustrate a *coniunctio oppositorum*.[†] They are in opposition but with a latent conjunction hidden within them, the basis of any union.[8] Like is joined to unlike, male to female, coming together in a synthesis resulting in the production of a family. Unions joining like to like, e.g., male to male or female to female, that is 'homosexual', are necessarily barren and are not accommodated in the coniunctio oppositorum but astrology makes provision for them elsewhere as will be seen later. Other ideas relevant here are Being and Not-Being, Self and Other, Identity and Difference, Independence and Interdependence, Singularity and Duality. In the logic of Hegel Identity and Difference contain each other within each other and are thus essentially the same. Self and Other are also two aspects of the same: as the Vedas have it, 'Tat Tvam Asi', 'thou art that'.[9] This explains why in astrology a planet in the seventh house, say Saturn, may indicate an external obstacle or difficulty in a partnership or alternatively an internal inhibition of 'hang-up' denied or rejected and *projected* onto the 'other'. The Descendant implies both acceptance and rejection at one and the same time. Between the two there is an 'enantiodromia', each side running into the other (Gk., 'enantios' = opposite, 'dromia' = running), an idea originated by the pre-Socratic philosopher Heraclitus of Ephesus, incorporated by Hegel into his philosophy and developed psychologically by Jung. 'Men do not understand', said Heraclitus, 'how that which is torn in different directions comes into accord with itself, "harmony in contrariety", an attunement of opposite tension as in the bow and the lyre'. This harmony in contrariety is a feature of both signs and houses, as if

---

[†] The opposition illustrated by the Ascendant and Descendant is paradoxical. Orthodox western thinking rests on Aristotelian logic, the law of identity, the law of contradiction, and that of the 'excluded middle'. Or rather it is an opposition in which Aristotelian thinking is replaced by, or develops into, that of the pre-Socratic Heraclitus of Ephesus and or oriental thinking as in Buddhism or Taoism. In Aristotle A is A (i.e., identity, 'conjunction', Ascendant), or A is not-A (i.e., contradiction, 'opposition', Descendant). In astrology the logic is paradoxical as in Eastern philosophies, Heraclitus and notably Hegel. Here A and not-A are not mutually exclusive, in which the third term is not the impossible excluded middle of orthodox logic but the paradoxical Hegelian synthesis and the 'harmony in contrariety' of Heraclitus. In the words of Chuang-tzu, 'that which is one is one, and that which is not-one is also one'. Related to this are Jung's 'enantiocromia', the 'coniunctio oppositorum' and the 'thou art that' of the Upanishads. This relates again to the 'projection' of modern psychology.

their unknown originator had known of Heraclitus and foreseen Hegel. Johannes Scheffler records the harmony in the following couplet:
> 'Der Mensch hat eher nicht vollkommne Seligkeit,
> Bis dass die Einheit hat verschluckt die Anderheit'.

(Man has not achieved complete bliss (or blessedness) until 'The One' has swallowed 'The Other'). In the dialectic each side swallows (verschluckt) the other and contains it within it. This inclusion of one within the other has a physical counterpart in the complementary structure of the human organs of generation where homologues of male organs are found within the female and homologues of the female within the male.

The interplay between the two poles of the Horizon - subject and object - is worked out in detail by Hegel. I quote from W.T. Stace (The Philosophy of Hegel, 1924). 'The object has now emerged from the *recesses* of the subject and taken up an independent position confronting it. It is this *independence* of the object which first gets recognition. The object is not-me, is something alien, in which I have no part. It is not yet realized that the object is, in its truth, only a projection of myself. It is at first seen as completely external, independent and alien from the subject, an absolute other over against it. This is the position of *consciousness proper*.'

This describes exactly the subject-object relationship in astrology considered as opposing poles of the Horizon, the Ascendant and Descendant. Note that the object is only a *projection* of oneself, though seen as external, independent and alien. The modern psychoanalytic theory of projection is seen portrayed in Hegel's philosophy two centuries ago and in astrology two millennia ago. Dr. Stace goes further into the relationship for another nine pages and, since most of it is relevant to the understanding of astrology it repays examination but we have no room for it here.

To go a little further, according to the dialectic subject and object, e.g., thesis and antithesis, run together, our of which comes a third term - synthesis, i.e., harmony. The passage of the one into the other does not involve time or causation. With the Horizon as the axis of presentational immediacy no time is involved. There is a curious analogy with Bell's[10] Theorem in sub-atomic physics. Bell's Theorem states that there is a connection between sub-atomic particles which is non-physical and moreover instantaneous. According to the laws of physics 'communication' requires a signal to go from one place to another and signals cannot go faster than light. In Bell's experiment the communication was faster than light, it was instantaneous. In a pair of particles if one has a spin 'up' the other always has a spin 'down'. If one particle changed from spin 'up' to spin 'down', the other changed from 'down' to 'up'. Not only was the change instantaneous, there was no physical link between the two. It was as if one particle knew exactly what the other was up to and each mirrored the other simultaneously. Bell's Theorem suggests that the two particles in instantaneous but a-physical connection are essentially two aspects of the same thing. It looks as though the structure and symbolism of astrology, the ideas of Heraclitus, Hegel and Jung together with Bell's Theorem all have a common origin. Bell's Theorem also suggests that not only are the two particles part of each other but that both are part of a greater whole in which all parts are somehow integrated, an idea again which is not alien to astrology. It suggests that what happens in one place is linked instantaneously with what happens elsewhere, anywhere in the universe. Parts are no longer separate parts but are intimately linked into an all-embracing whole. The analogy is striking, with the physical world of quantum mechanics mirroring the rational world as revealed in the dialectic.

Apart from the logic of interaction each house suggests a direction of interest and sometimes of occupation. The first house being the leader of the twelve from which the others take their tune is in one sense more general than the others since it, in the Ascendant, acts as filter or focus through which the meanings of the rest are coloured and qualified. In another sense it is more personal than the others and indicative of the type of body or mind of the subject. As leader it suggests independent occupations requiring initiative, aggressiveness and daring, especially if occupied by Mars or the Sun. The seventh house, on the other hand, suggests close association with others and occupations requiring deliberative assessment and balanced appreciation especially when tenanted by Venus. Art appreciation, assessors, marriage guidance counsellors, referees, the judiciary, equal rights protagonists, advocates, diplomats and organizers of social events are a few such examples.

THE SECOND HOUSE   Associated sign Taurus

This underlies and supports the first house and was known to the Greeks as *Bios*, life. Instead of the primitive impulse of the first house we have the primitive need for sustenance and support, the necessity for taking in material for the maintenance of life. Whereas the first house is outgoing the second is in-taking. Grasping, taking in and storing up are the ideas to be borne in mind, whether physically, emotionally or mentally. Food, money and property are taken in and stored up as are also sensations and feelings, both as physical insurance and protection and as psychological support. The needs of the senses. Sensual appreciation, sensuality, one's inner feelings, a desire for creature comforts and appreciation of the good things of life. More particularly financial standing, money, movable property and possessions (landed property comes under the fourth house), income and earnings all come under this house. Related to the sign Taurus it is an index of stability or alternatively or inertia. Institutions and occupations related to this house are: Builders, construction firms, building societies, banks, insurance houses, pension funds, earned capital, stocks and shares, food stores, depositories, warehouses, 'wine lakes and sugar mountains', collectors, art dealers, acoustics experts, ear, nose and throat specialists, dietitians and dentists, upholsterers and interior decorators. The rationale for the above may not in all cases be immediately evident but will become so when we come to the zodiacal signs.

THE EIGHTH HOUSE   Associated sign - Scorpio

Where the second house is concerned with taking in for oneself, the eighth relates to giving out to, or receiving from, others. Ingestion is replaced by excretion and elimination. The elimination, paying out or disbursement is however two-sided. In traditional astrology this sector is concerned, among other things, with the ideas of sex and death; indeed the Greek name for it was *Thanatos* (death) opposing and complementing the *Bios* (life) of the second house while the sex of the eighth is reflected in the sensuality of the second. The one-sided aspect of the second is opposed to the two-sided aspect of the eighth. Sex inevitably involves another, one's incidental opposite, whereas sensuality need not, and in sex one loses oneself in the other, in the 'coniunctio', so that sex is in a sense a sort of death. Giving and receiving, sex, self-elimination and death are basic ideas here. Psychologically if the second house suggests emotional block, the eighth suggests catharsis. Another idea associated with the eighth house is that of regeneration, a reflection on a spiritual level of the physically generative quality of the house. Regeneration may be a sequel to psychological catharsis.

Instead of harbouring one's physical or psychological resources (second house) here one is prepared to exhaust them. Self-preservation is replaced by a willingness for self-sacrifice. On a more mundane level this house is considered to relate to the management and control of property and finance, not earned but received through others or in co-operation with others, or to the property of others in which one has an interest. Income through others, disbursement, wills and legacies, i.e., receiving from others as a result of death, all come under this house. This sector, analogous with the sign Scorpio, is associated with the planets Mars and Pluto. Institutions and occupations with this house are demolition firms, tax officials, pawnbrokers and moneylenders, agents of death and bankruptcy, e.g., undertakers and receivers, bailiffs, agents of catharsis, e.g., psychiatrists, and of physical reconstruction, e.g., surgeons, those concerned with sex and generation - geneticists, infertility specialists, venereologists, urologists, immunologists, AIDS specialists, plumbers and sewerage contractors. Agents of spiritual regeneration - gurus and healers.

THE THIRD HOUSE   Associated sign - Gemini

This house makes the first break in the self-centredness implied by the first two, indicating a capacity for relationship, though the relationship has nevertheless a self-centred core. Here, however, there is a need to communicate with others, even if only in one's own interests. The first three houses, like the first three signs, are all predominantly self-centred. They can be seen embodying the ideas of 'action' (first), 'feeling' (second) and 'thought' (third), and as representing symbolically the first requirements of primitive man - hunting and killing (Aries, first), the establishment of agriculture, gathering and storing (Taurus, second), and communication, gesticulation, language and speech (Gemini, third).

To the Greeks this house was known as *Thea* (goddess) which we may interpret as the goddess of reason. It relates to our innate structured reasoning capacity. Here we see symbolized the birth of language as an instrument of communication. This house, which is associated with the sign Gemini and its ruler Mercury,[11] lies below the Horizon and adjacent to the Lower Heaven signifying inheritance. The idea that the structure of language is innate, foreshadowed in Plato's Meno, has been championed in modern times by Professor Noam Chomsky in his 'Syntactic Structures'. There has since been further support for this from a number of psychologists. If, indeed, Chomsky and his school are proved right then we have here yet another instance in which the structure of astrology and its associated meaning appear to accord with the fact. The ruler of the third sign, Mercury (Gk. Hermes) is commemorated in the word 'hermeneutics', i.e., the art of interpretation. This house embraces the whole field of language and criticism. Structuralists, constructionists and de-constructionists in linguistics such as Saussure, Derrida and others find their place here. As we have noted the third house is adjacent to the Lower Heaven, the 'Arche' signifying origins. Derrida even calls his de-constructionism 'archi-écriture'.

Logic and mathematics come under this house and such activities as speaking, writing, lecturing, teaching, theoretical work, the use of words, numbers, signs and codes to convey meaning. Both intellectual and manual dexterity, skill and instrumentation find their place here, though not so much as learned skills and expertise as inherited talent. Learned expertise relates to the sixth house and the sign Virgo. Musicians as well as writers are represented here but as talented instrumentalists rather than as composers, and the writers here are more likely journalists than original authors. Creativity and originality come under the fifth and eleventh houses. Technology as an extension of manual dexterity and logical application may also be referred to this house, the development and employment of instruments of communication, language, newspapers, telephone, radio and television being examples. Communication also involves movement from place to place so that walking, driving, commuting and all forms of vehicular transport, regular travel and short journeys fall into this house. This is also the intellectual home of Aristotle's *peripatetics* - 'discitur ambulando'.[12]

Commerce and interchange (Mercury was the god of commerce, as also of thieves) are represented here - markets, bureaux de change, travel agents, railways, bus services and air lines. Education, teaching and instruction, schools, seminaries, technical colleges and apprentice workshops all come within this sector.

In traditional astrology this house signifies close relations such as siblings and neighbours, i.e., relationships not chosen by the subject but arising out of the circumstances in which one is placed. Chosen relationships - wives, husbands, lovers, partners relate to the seventh house, while others less intimate, friends and acquaintances correspond to the eleventh house. The third house adjoins the Lower Heaven representing not only heredity but also the home, so that it is a logical place for neighbours (close to home) and for brothers and sisters (part of home and inheritance). The seventh house, on the other hand, adjoins the Descendant representing one's chosen milieu, choice and free-will relating to the Horizon, so that the assignment of siblings to the third and partners to the seventh fits in with the inherent logic.

THE NINTH HOUSE   Associated sign - Sagittarius

This was known to the Greeks as *Theos* (God) and it complements the third house's *Thea*. If Thea refers to the Goddess of Reason, Theos corresponds to the God of Wisdom, Zeus or Jupiter, and indeed the house is related analogically with the ninth sign Sagittarius, the sign of Jupiter. In Greek mythology Zeus' first wife was Metis (Goddess of Wisdom), so we have Jupiter and Metis representing Sagittarius and Gemini, the ninth and third houses, coming together in a coniunctio oppositorum. This synthesis resulted in the birth of Athena Parthenos represented in the sign of Virgo and the sixth house, 'parthenos' being the Greek word for virgin. The sixth house is in square or 90° aspect with both the third and ninth houses, and here we have an instance of the right-angle symbolizing generation. The conjunction is a 'nominative' aspect grammatically, the opposition an 'accusative' aspect, while the square is a 'genitive' aspect, an angle of 'generation'. For example the fourth house is in square to both first and seventh, and their union (first 'proposal') (seventh 'acceptance') results in pregnancy and birth related symbolically with Cancer and the fourth house. Such combinations of geometry with symbolism enable us to relate one set of concepts with another, in this case mythology with human potential.

In the ninth house short term exploitation is replaced by long term aim. In the third house interests are nearer at hand; in the ninth they are extended to full stretch. Logic is expanded to speculative thinking; the mind takes a leap and tends to explore more remote and theoretical subjects such as philosophy and religion, or seeks to develop ideas inherent in the third, or promulgate them to a wider public. Here the accuracy of the third may be sacrificed to reach the precision to depth. More distant, more elevated goals are envisaged; learning is less factual, more exploratory and imaginative. This is the house of the higher grades of learning and of the professions, and it is noteworthy that in Dr. Gauquelin's statistical researches this house was repeatedly emphasized in the horoscopes of academics of note. If the third house can be related to Aristotle's peripatetic Lyceum, the ninth may similarly symbolize Plato's Academy. The coniunctio oppositorum here (Plato - Aristotle) gave birth to western philosophy represented in the sixth house and the sign Virgo, opposed to eastern philosophy with its mystical content in the opposite and esoteric sign Pisces. Here again we see the generative right-angle operative, this time in the Groves of Academe.

In traditional astrology the ninth house was said to represent the 'higher mind' since it combines reason with imagination. In Whitehead's philosophy such speculative reason is called 'higher appetition', the desire for better things. If the third house represents the student, the ninth stands for the postgraduate, doctor or professor. If the third represents the journalist, the ninth stands for the writer or author, or his publisher. Here is meant the old-style publisher prepared to publish for literary value not the new-style governed by market value, which latter could better be accommodated in the third house.

Like the third house the ninth is connected with movement and travel, but here the movement is more extended, the distances greater. Routine movement from place to place here becomes purposeful travel possibly involving foreign countries, also the exploration of remote areas. There is a desire to reach further both with mind and body. Long distance aims rather than more immediate interests are the spur to activity. If the third house relates to schools, the ninth embraces universities, institutes of learning and colleges of further education, academics and scholars, explorers and travellers. In the spiritual field it relates to religious exegesis, ministers of religion and religious leaders as also to places of worship.

In the sporting field it has to do with long distance pursuits such as hunting and long distance running.

THE FOURTH HOUSE   Associated sign - Cancer

The cusp of the fourth house is formed by the Lower Heaven. This house is traditionally connected with childhood, home life, family, parents and upbringing, conception and birth. It is associated with beginnings, the past, inheritance, the accumulation of past experiences and memory.[13] It stands, among other things, for what we have left behind us and yet still carry with us as accumulated experience. It is linked to its neighbour, the third house, by the Lower Meridian representing Arche, beginnings, but whereas the third relates to mental origins the fourth refers to physical origins, to first causes rather than first principles.

The fourth house relates to the individual's attitude to his roots, to the home, place of birth, country of birth, familial and tribal tradition and custom. Mars or Uranus in this house in discordant aspect may suggest the rebel against the family, or the rejection of, or break with, one origins. Saturn here may relate to the weight of parental authority, to oppression in childhood from whatever source, or alternatively frugality in the home, or possible obstinacy. Jupiter here suggests generous parents and possibly a spoilt childhood. Alternatively it may indicate generosity to one's own children and great enjoyment in family life with little spared in the cuisine or the welcome.

This house is associated with the soil, the hearth, mother earth, the womb from which all things spring. In contrast to its neighbour the third it is concerned not with reason but with instinct, imagination, emotion and memory. Caring, nurturing and hospitality find their place here as does also pregnancy and post-natal care. In its more material aspect the house relates to property, not the movable property of the second house but inherited property, landed property, real estate, houses, bases and foundations. We have mentioned that the fourth house is connected with parenthood. Traditional astrology is split in two on this point, some authorities assigning the father to the fourth, others the mother. If, however, we follow the inherent logic of astrology it is evident that the fourth house should relate to the closer, more caring parent, usually the mother while the more remote, more authoritative parent, usually the father (though not necessarily so) is located in the opposite house, the tenth. In the case of one-parent families the parent, of whichever sex, may be indicated in both fourth and tenth houses. Which parent is seen as the more authoritative or the more caring may differ between children of the same family. Associated also with this house are places of birth, ancestral homes, base camps, shelters, caves, ships, vessels and receptacles, maternity homes, nurseries, creches and children's homes, also nurses, nannies, midwives, child care workers, obstetricians, gynaecologists, estate agents, land stewards, antique dealers, potters and shipwrights.

THE TENTH HOUSE   Associated sign - Capricorn

The cusp of this house is formed by the Midheaven and traditionally it is connected with aims and goals, achievement, success, public life, authority and control. In contrast to its opposite the fourth house it refers to the future, to possibilities and opportunities, to anticipations, aspirations and projects. If the fourth house relates to origins the tenth concerns ends, while the first and seventh suggest means. The end aimed at is the summit of achievement. It is, so to speak, the magnet, the lodestone drawing us upwards and forwards from our origins to the peak of our capabilities. The arrow of time starts in the Lower Heaven and finds its target in the Midheaven,[14] travelling from Arche, beginnings, to Telos, ends. While the fourth house suggests the push from behind, the stick to the donkey, the individual driven by instinct and inheritance, the tenth illustrates the pull from in front, the carrot to the donkey, the drawing power of aims, ambitions and aspirations.

Public standing, reputation, recognition and career are represented in the tenth, as aims whether fulfilled or not. This house also stands for the subject's attitude to authority, to his employers, superiors or elders. The planet indirectly associated with this house is Saturn, complementing the Moon associated with the fourth. Saturn is also symbolic of the father as the Moon is of the mother. Here the father is seen as paternal law-giver, disciplinarian and sometimes object of fear. Occasionally Saturn may relate to the mother, especially in a single parent family where the mother may have to take over the role of disciplinarian as well as carer. The other side of fatherhood, the closer more intimate, warmer and more playful and outgoing side is represented by the Sun.

The tenth and its preceding house, the ninth, bestride the Midheaven. Both relate to future aspirations, to purpose, to aims and development, but whereas the ninth concerns mental achievement the tenth relates to physical, tangible, practical goals. The aims of the tenth are concerned with high office and public recognition while those of the ninth relate to 'higher appetition', the search for personal self-betterment philosophically or religiously. The tenth is material, the ninth mental or intellectual.

The Meridian linking the fourth and the tenth and the Horizon connecting the first and seventh house illustrate the conflict between ends and means, between heredity and environment, between time and space, between function and structure and between principle and pragmatism. The structure of astrology provides us with co-ordinates for relating ideas in a coherently logical way. In astrology the tenth house is second only to the first in importance, the primacy of the first being due to the fact that the 'here and now' and not the 'there and then' is the locus of all manifestation. In the words of St. Augustine of Hippo, 'there be three times; the present of things past, the present of things present, and the present of things future'. Nothing occurs, nothing materializes except in the present symbolized by the Horizon.

The tenth house relates to authorities of all kinds, to 'father figures', parental role models, to Freud's 'super-ego', to controllers, regulators, lawyers, law enforcement officers, police, governors, directors, managers, superiors, indeed all invested with some sort of authority. Government buildings, ministries, law courts, edifices and monuments of prestige and honour also come under this house.

THE FIFTH HOUSE   Associated sign - Leo

This house was known to the Greeks as Agathe Tyche (good fortune). The fundamental meaning here is that of self-expression in its creative aspect. It symbolizes the direction which the individual's urge to create, propagate and express himself to the full, will tend to follow. Ideas associated with this house are expressive of forms of enjoyment, desire, love, erotic play, sport, adventure, risk, drama, demonstration, display and artistic creativity. It has to do with free-play, both of mind and body, in which the constraints of home (fourth house) and of career (tenth) are broken and the subject does what he really wants to do and, if still constrained, what he does with his free time. While the seventh house has to do with marriage and union, the fifth may be considered as a sort of prelude to it, standing for the period of courtship and engagement while the options are still open. It may also stand for free love, for affairs, for periods of limited co-habitation, for mistress or lover. Permanent co-habitation as in marriage refers to the seventh house. The seventh implies explicit or tacit agreement or contract, the fifth adventure and risk. It represents the free expression of the libido, the philoprogenitive urge and its consequences - children. Here, however, in contrast to the precedent fourth house, children are regarded not so much as members of the family to be protected, but rather as independent beings in themselves. The emphasis is on play and freedom rather than on care and protection. In the fourth house the child is seen as a dependent member of the family, the creature of a certain inheritance to which it is inescapably bound, the fourth house being adjacent to the Lower Heaven symbolizing heredity. If the fifth the child is its own person with its own life to live. Associated with the fifth house is the Sun, ruler of the fifth sign, Leo, and much of the warmth and splendour of the Sun is recognizable in the characteristics with which this house is associated. Saturn, however, in the fifth suggests a serious, cool, inhibited or frustrated, or calculatingly persistent attitude to the affairs indicated. Neptune here may indicate, idealized or Platonic love, secretive affairs or, on the other hand, a loose, permissive attitude with no holds barred. Uranus here suggests the possibility of unusual, compulsive attractions such as a compelling fascination for someone unusual, perhaps of different class, race, colour or religious persuasion, or alternatively for someone of the same sex, i.e., homosexuality. It may also indicate the possibility of unusual or talented children. In the wider world the creativity of the fifth house may manifest itself in drama, showmanship, music, authorship or art. The impresario and the symphony conductor are typical examples as also the actor and show-business personality. Film directors, business organisers and managers, entrepreneurs, speculators, tycoons, celebrities and notabilities all relate to the fifth house. Institutions so connected are theatres, opera houses, amphitheatres, art galleries, amusement parks, safari parks, sports grounds, stadia, race courses and fair grounds.

THE ELEVENTH HOUSE   Associated sign - Aquarius

Known to the Greeks as Agathos Daimon (good spirit) it opposes and complements the Agathe Tyche of the fifth and, like it, has been traditionally regarded as a fortunate house. Here, however, we have not so much physical creativity as intellectual creativity association and invention. The association of ideas on the mental level is reflected in association with others on the social plane. In traditional astrology this is often called the 'house of friends' for the relationship here indicated is less vital or emotional than the erotic, romantic relationship implied by its opposite, the fifth, and tends to be sublimated. Even the friends are acquaintances rather than intimates for the association denoted is a loose one and is entered into for personal reasons on an impersonal plane with no intention of emotional involvement. The orientation, then, is more detached, the association freely made and freely broken, for freedom is as essential, or indeed more essential than in the fifth.

There is an element of idealism here, a desire to get together and associate with others for the common good, not so much an immediate practical good but rather an ideal located somewhere in the future - an utopian ideal. Karl Marx had the eleventh sign Aquarius on the Ascendant and the revolutionary planet Uranus and the idealist planet Neptune in his eleventh house. Marxism foundered on the rocks of intractable human nature, a not unusual fate for Utopian schemes. The eleventh house has often been termed the home of 'hopes and wishes'. It could, on occasion, merit the epithet, the house of broken hopes and shattered wishes.

As with the third and seventh houses the eleventh is concerned with intercommunication. These three 'Air' houses form within the horoscope an equilateral triangle of communication. In the third it is the simpler, more routine, concrete aspects that are emphasized. In the seventh we have the idea or reciprocity and interchange, mutuality and complement, but in the eleventh the field is widened still further though in a more detached, theoretical sense than in the other two houses. Intimate friends, like pet ideas, find their place in the seventh house; remoter friends and vast ideas are found in the eleventh. Relationships in the eleventh may breach the bounds of convention and ideas may be related to other ideas which on the face of it have no connection whatever. Hence the capacity for discovery and invention which is a feature of both house and its associated sign,

Aquarius. Aquarius is associated with two contrasting planets, Saturn (convention) and Uranus (unconventionality) and this contrast is also manifest in the eleventh house, the Saturnine flint sparking Ukranian originality. Here the rational and irrational aspects of the planets may combine to heuristic effect. Uranus is considered to be a higher octave of Mercury, to transcend its logic through 'lateral thinking'. Invention is often the result of looking athwart at convention, i.e., 'pour inventer il fault penser à côté'.† Theorists, theoretical physicists, theoretical politicians, democrats, utopians, eccentrics, inventors, people of original ideas and of hare-brained schemes, cranks, ideologists, humanists, agnostics, nuclear scientists, specialists in upper motor neurone disease, organizers of clubs and associations, committee men, scientists in electro-magnetism, electricians, TV technicians and brain surgeons. Clubs, associations, societies, groups freely formed for specific purposes, democratic institutions, discussion groups, debating societies and committees all find their place here. If the tenth house is the house of government the eleventh is the house of parliament.

THE SIXTH HOUSE   Associated sign - Virgo

This was known to the Greeks as Kake Tyche (ill fortune). Traditionally known as the house of work, service and health it refers to the day to day functioning of the physical body as well as one's daily bread-winning work in the world. It relates to the subjects attitude to disciplined routine, subordinate work of any kind and refers to him as a subordinate and to others who may be subordinate to him. All forms of specialized service from menial jobs to service in the community, social service, welfare and health services, the armed services, police, the civil service, work in the service of a firm or of the state, or of authority, come under this house. Here the police are seen as servants of the public, not as repressive authority as in the tenth house. The efficient routine

---

† Karl Popper claims that there is no such thing as 'a logical method of having new ideas' and that 'every discovery contains an irrational element or a creative intuition'. (The Logic of Scientific Discovery', p. 32). Einstein, too, asserted that there was no logical path leading to 'highly universal laws'. 'They can only be reached by intuition'. (Einstein's address on Max Planck's 60th birthday).

running of a business finds its place here, as also the efficient physiological functioning of the body machine - hence the connection with health, for just as the individual may be considered as in the service of the community so are the individual cells of the body in service to the whole. If the subject has a tendency to some functional derangement one may sometimes get a clue to its nature from the sixth house and any planet within it. Sometimes a clue to psycho-somatic trouble may be obtained here. Accident or injury does not relate to this house but to the poles of the Horizon, the Ascendant and Descendant, the immediacy of an accident corresponding with the implications of the Horizon. Organic trouble, on the other hand, would appear to relate to the eighth house.

The third house as we have already remarked is the locus of inherited skills and aptitudes since it adjoins the lower Meridian representing heredity; the sixth, however, relates to learned skills and acquired expertise since it adjoins the Descendant representing environment and circumstance. We have here two aspects of the common ruler, Mercury. The former, represented by the positive sign Gemini and the third house, is a positive manoeuvre since the subject projects an innate talent onto whatever concerns him. The latter illustrated by the sixth house and the negative sign Virgo, gains or learns his expertise from contact with his milieu or from others which could be described as a negative aspect or function. Here, once again we see the basic ideas of house, sign and polarity conforming to the geometry of meaning inherent in the horoscope.

Doctors, health workers, health services, technicians, craftsmen, chemists, pathologists, apprentices, analysts, civil servants, pupils, draughtsmen, mechanics, critics, workers in professions requiring discriminating mental work of skilful hand-work, servants, school-teachers. Institutions include surgeries, clinics, pharmacies, laboratories, workshops, training centres, craft centres, ateliers, studios, precision instrument firms and medical suppliers.

THE TWELFTH HOUSE   Associated sign - Pisces

The last house of the twelve was called by the Greeks Kakos Daimon (evil spirit). Like the sixth it was considered an unfortunate house. The misfortune attributed to both these houses appears to refer to their being ill-placed from the point of view of material benefit or gain rather than of anything intrinsically disastrous. The subordinate occupations of the sixth and the personal withdrawnness of the twelfth are not conducive to the rapid acquisition of wealth and many astrologers in the past, as also our acquisitive society of today, seem to have been obsessed with money. The orientation of the twelfth is toward solitude, quiet, work on one's own, secrecy, seclusion - a desire to get away from the world, or toward enforced seclusion by law (imprisonment), or by physical or mental ill-health (hospitalisation), or other misfortune. Whereas the sixth house indicates material involvement with one's environment whether in nervous reaction to it or in work itself, the twelfth stands for the self involved with the psyche. The sixth house is in the 'other-oriented' hemisphere of the horoscope adjoining the Descendant and it concerns a functional relationship with the environment. The twelfth house is in the self-centred half and is subjective, bent back on itself, introspective and self-preoccupied. Both the twelfth and the first houses adjoin the Ascendant and both have therefore a subjective implication, but where the first looks outward the twelfth looks inward. The first is self-opinionated, the twelfth self-conscious, the first physically active, the twelfth mentally receptive.

Like the eleventh house the twelfth embraces a modicum of unconventionality. The fist ten houses represents the average person's spectrum of normality. The last two, however, associated with the ultre-Saturnian planets Uranus and Neptune have more than a touch of originality about them and are in some way unusual, exceptional, sometimes a little eccentric or highly original (Uranus - Aquarius), or rather otherworldly (Neptune - Pisces). The eleventh house is the home of the nervous and highly strung (Uranus), the twelfth of the hypersensitive and ill-co-ordinated (Neptune). In this last house the individual isolates himself, or is isolated, from the material world and takes refuge in the mind. Materially it is the most restricted sector of all and under this heading one can list places of restraint - Prisons, asylums, hospitals, monasteries, homes for the sick and disabled, the indigent or the mentally disturbed, the monk's cell, the hermit's cave, the academic's study and the psychologist's couch. Mentally, however, there is no restriction for the mind is more free here than in any other house. There is no limit to its range for the restriction is a purely material one. The unconventionality of the eleventh and twelfth houses is, however, often not marked or even noticeable for each is associated with a conventional planet to balance the maverick - the eleventh has Saturn to balance Uranus while the twelfth has Jupiter to balance Neptune. Many planets in the twelfth house may indicate an interest in the subconscious mind, psychology, the paranormal and extra-sensory perception, or an orientation toward imaginative work, abstract ideas or metaphysics. The reference to imagination and abstraction combined with great mental scope and work in seclusion may go some way to explain why in Dr. Gauquelin's statistical researches this house, together with the ninth was repeatedly emphasized in the horoscopes of those prominent in the learned professions.

It will be seen later that these indications of the roles of the houses are reflected at a deeper level in the meanings of the signs of the zodiac. While the houses relate to present circumstances the signs are concerned with congenital potentials and proclivities. The meanings of the signs become orientated in the direction of the houses in which the rotation of the earth places them and the meanings of the circumstantial houses are coloured by the congenital significance of the signs. Sometimes it is difficult to give priority to one over the other and in all cases the significance of both should be taken into consideration and balanced against each other.

The circle of houses is of increasing complexity and, now that we have completed it, it will be seen that there is a certain connecting thread or nexus of meaning discoverable in each and peculiar to it while yet being in significant relationship not only with its opposite and neighbour but with those basic structures, the Meridian and Horizon. Cassirer's claim that the crossing of these two diameters provides us with a framework for understanding, a basic schema of co-ordinates for interpreting our involvement in our world, is apparently fulfilled. A similar logic and coherence is discoverable in the oppositions, quadratures and triangulations of the signs of the zodiac.

IV. THE ELEMENTS

'His life was gentle, and the elements
So mix'd in him that Nature might stand up
And say to all the world, "This was a man!"'.

(Julius Caesar)

Vier Elemente, innig gesellt
Bilden das Leben, bauen die Welt.[1]

(Schiller)

Wenn du den Schöpfer hast, so läuft dir alles nach,
Mensch, Engel, Sonn, and Mond, Luft, Feuer, Erd und Bach.[2]

(Angelus Silesius)

The precise origin of the doctrine of the elements - Fire, Air, Water and Earth - is in doubt, but probably Indian. It was introduced, however, to the west by the philosopher-physician Empedocles of Acragas to be taken up later by Plato. In astrology the elements are seen as filters or screens through which meaning is qualified, whether by means of planetary symbols or structural co-ordinates, the Ascendant, Midheaven, etc. Psychologically they may be seen as indicators of temperament, e.g. a 'fiery temperament', but they may also be regarded more widely. Temperament itself may have other connotations. The psychologist Kretschmer, for instance, regarded it as 'ein heuristisches Kennwort', a pointer for discovery.

The four elements relate roughly to the four 'humours' - choleric (Fire), sanguine (Air), phlegmatic (Water) and melancholic (Earth). The German psychologist Wilhelm Wundt divided the homours into strong and weak, fast and slow, as follows - choleric (strong and fast), sanguine (weak and fast), phlegmatic (weak and slow), melancholic (strong and slow). In astrological symbolism the above can be tabulated as follows:

Fire: strong and rapid feeling response. (Aries, Leo, Sagittarius).
Air: weak but rapid feeling response. (Libra, Aquarius, Gemini).
Water: weak, slow feeling response. (Cancer, Scorpio, Pisces).
Earth: strong, slow feeling response. (Capricorn, Taurus, Virgo).

In Plato's cosmology the elements relate to the 'perfect solids', the tetrahedron (Fire), the octahedron (Air), the icosahedron (Water) and the hexahedron (Earth). Plato himself refers to the elements as *ta stoicheia* which can be translated as 'first principles', but they are to be understood not a things but as qualities and Plato expressly states so. Since the elements are 'universals', which we can describe as Fire-like, Air-like, Water-like and Earth-like generally, they can be applied as such in a variety of differing fields. They can, for instance, symbolize different states of matter in which Earth stands for the solid state, Water for the fluid state, Air for the gaseous state and Fire for the electric or combustive state. If Earth, Water and Air relate to the molecular level, then Fire relates to the atomic level. Fire and Air are positive elements, faster and more active; they tend to rise upward and spread outward. Water and Earth are negative, slower and passive; they tend to fall, run together and collect in the lowest level (Water) or condense (Earth). Suppose we arrange them in a table:

FIRE	+ Fastest, Hottest, Lightest. Combustion	Activity
AIR	+ Fast, Warm, Light. Vaporisation	↓ ↑
WATER	− Slow, Cool, Heavy. Liquefaction	
EARTH	− Slowest, Coldest, Heaviest. Solidification	Inertia

The same first principles are manifested at all levels. Even at the mundane level of, say, heating a house, electricity we can see would come under the rubric Fire, gas under Air, oil under Water, and coal under Earth. What we are doing here is assigning 'particulars' to 'universals' and one can see at once that it presents little difficulty. When, however, we come to consider the psychological import of the elements we have to take into account the four 'humours' as well. Aristotle applied the principles Hot, Cold, Wet and Dry to the four elements in the following way, as also does astrology:

Fire: Hot and Dry
Air: Warm and Moist
Water: Cool and Wet
Earth: Cold and Dry

The Hot and Dry were considered active qualities; the Cold and Wet were passive. Fire, then, was doubly active, Air combined active and passive, so did Earth, while Water was doubly passive. The result of this is that in the horoscope, where Fire opposes Air and

Earth opposes Water across the zodiacal circle, although in the first case both signs are positive Fire is always the active partner to Air, and in the second where both signs are negative Earth is the active partner to Water. There is an exception here, however, in the Taurus - Scorpio polarity since the active Earth sign is associated with the passive planet Venus while the passive Water sign is associated with the active Mars so that the sign opposition is brought into harmony by the complementary planetary opposition. Since, in astrology, one of the psychological connotations of positivity is extroversion, of negativity introversion, we now have a rearrangement of our previous table in which Fire is seen as the most extrovert, Water the most introvert.

FIRE:	Positive/Active	Extrovert
AIR:	Positive/Passive	↓ ↑
EARTH:	Negative/Active	
WATER:	Negative/Passive	Introvert

In the circle of the horoscope each of the four elements is linked to its fellows by 'trine aspects' (120 degrees), see diagram p. 55, so that the four form a series of equilateral triangles or 'triplicities'. We have the twelve signs arranged in threes and fours. This three-four arrangement is reversed in a further arrangement of 'qualities' in terms of movement. Here each of the three qualities is linked to its fellows by 'square aspects' (90 degrees), see diagram, in what are known as 'quadruplicities'. The qualities, related to the three Indian 'Gunas' are as follows: Cardinal (Initiating), Fixed (Perpetuating) and Mutable (Completing).

Cardinal: Initiating activity. Engagement with environment whether material or social. Positive cardinal signs incline to action and initiative; negative cardinals seek action and initiative. Kinetic energy. Applied force. Geometrical analogy - Linear. The straight line. Particle-wave analogy - the electron as particle.

Fixed: Latent energy which may appear as inertia or mass. The steady, persistent exercise of power, coupled with resistance to change. Cardinal energy is, as it were, stretched out, fluid, a current. Fixed energy is 'thickened', closely packed. It has the rotational energy of a vortex or dynamo. It gives form and an element of stability. A top, of itself, is essentially unstable, but if spun rapidly it will not only remain upright but will resist attempts to upset its equilibrium. A shapeless fluid attains form through rotation - a whirlpool. Even the air may assume a definite form in a whirlwind or cyclone. Fixed signs have the potential energy of a coiled spring. People with fixed signs emphasized tend to set up a relatively stable environment, embed themselves in it and hold on to it, but there is latent power behind the stability and the coiled spring may suddenly uncoil with dramatic results. Latent rotational energy tied to one spot. The key word is 'spin'. Geometrical analogy - the spiral. In physics - the nucleus of the atom.

Mutable: Variable energy. Diffuse, disseminated energy. Intermittent or variable application of force. Free movement, change. Adaptability, versatility, instability. Where Cardinals initiate and Fixed signs stabilize and control, Mutables elaborate and refine, adapt and complete. Lability and restlessness. Here the tendency is not so much to alter or control conditions as to observe them, adapt to them, or escape from them and seek new fields. The energy manifests itself in physical or mental restlessness, movement from place to place. Rhythmic motion. Free moving, variable force. Alternating or intermittent energy. The harmonics of motion, vibration, oscillation. Save motion. Geometrical analogy - the sinus curve. In physics - the electron in its wave form.

Those with Cardinal signs emphasized tend to be 'do-ers' and initiators. Those with Fixed signs prominent tend to be 'getters', 'havers' and preservers. Those with Mutable signs stressed tend to be 'changers', or to seek professions or services. Perhaps the simplest way of describing the difference is as follows:

> Cardinal: Changing, disturbing, unsettling others.
> Fixed: Unchanging, undisturbed, settled.
> Mutable: Changeable, disturbed, unsettled by others.

In the above we have a framework of meaning logically derived from geometrical position in the circle of the zodiac. The four elements, the triplicities, are in unconstrained relationship since the trine aspect (120°) contains no opposition and like is linked to like. The three modes,[3] the quadruplicities, relate to a different relationship since they contain both oppositions (180°) and squares (90°). In this sense the latter is the more dynamic relationship since energy is needed to overcome the difficulty while in the former there is little need for exertion. The inference is that someone with a predominance of factors in the modes may have a stressful life whereas one with an emphasis in the elements may find life relatively stress-free. Stress in Cardinal signs tends to work itself out in action and initiation, in Fixed signs to get bogged down or repressed psychologically, or result in stubborn intractability, and in Mutable signs to resolve itself in restless movement or intellectual activity.

Three x Four = Twelve

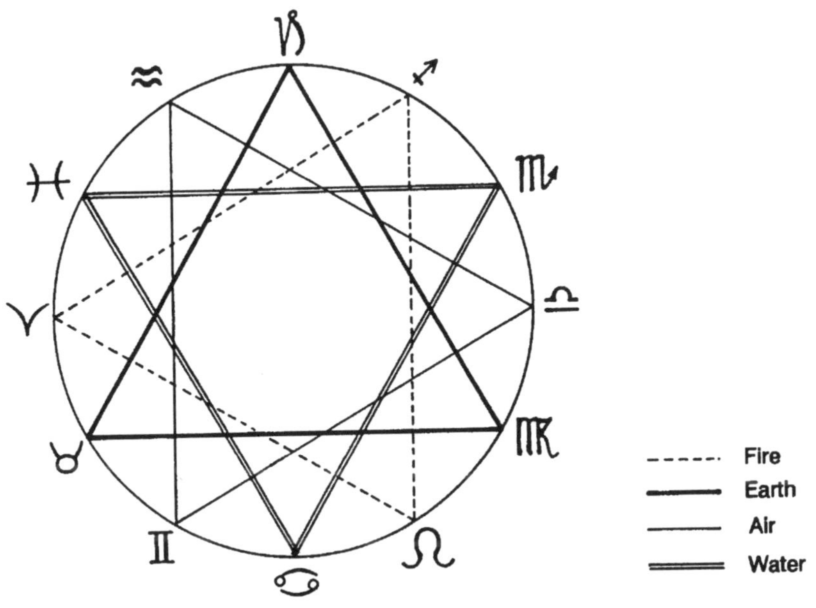

Figure 9 - The Triplicities (Three Groups of Four of Four Elements)

Plus is joined to plus.

Three x Four = Twelve

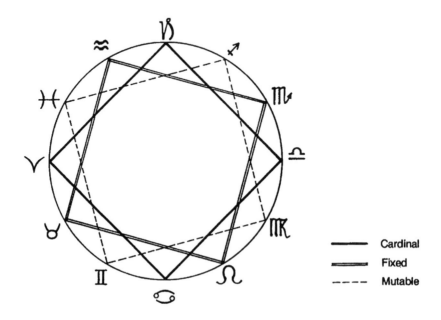

Figure 10 - The Quadrupliciities (Four Groups of Three Modes or Qualities)

Plus is joined to minus.

Before we proceed to further relationships let us look at a few more attributes of the elements, not in any exhaustive sense but merely as an illustration of the way in which qualities are seen to fall under the appropriate rubric.

	FIRE	AIR	WATER	EARTH
Manner:	*Expansion* *Radiation* *Giving* *Extravagant* *Egotistic* *Pushing*	*Diffusion* *Convection* *Distributing* *Equable* *Communicative* *Sociable*	*Collection* *Reflection* *Collecting* *Quiet* *Receptive* *Retiring*	*Contraction* *Absorbtion* *Retaining* *Restrained* *Stiff* *Off-hand*
Speech:	*Forceful* *Florid* *Exaggerative* *Personal*	*Fluent* *Connected* *Rational* *Explanatory*	*Rambling* *Subtle* *Imaginative* *Reflective*	*Dry* *Laconic* *Matter of fact* *Pedestrian*
Amplitude of Intellect:	*Singlemindedness*	*Breadth*	*Depth*	*Narrowness,* *Concentration*
Belief:	*Trust in self or in luck*	*Open mind*	*Belief, Superstition*	*Distrust,* *Scepticism*
Physical tone:	*Tense, taut, springy*	*Loose, free*	*Relaxed, slack*	*Stiff, firm*
Self-protection: Risk: Social Attitude:	*Attacking* *Rashness* *Aggressive* *Demanding* *Spirited type*	*Averting* *Calculated risk* *Expansive,* *Friendly,* *Thinking type*	*Hiding* *Imaginary fears* *Receptive* *Welcoming* *Feeling type*	*Withstanding* *Caution, Security* *Defensive* *Off-putting* *Practical type*

What we are doing here is assigning particular qualities to the relevant universals and once the symbolism is understood this presents little difficulty whether we are talking of the physical field, the mental, social or whatever. It should be obvious, for instance, that 'height' should relate to Fire, 'depth' to Water, while 'breadth' is represented by Air (expanded space) and Earth (contracted space).

To return to the Modes for a moment. On the extroversion-introversion scale Cardinals tend toward extroversion, Mutables toward introversion, Fixed toward the middle ground. This presents us with a difficulty for we have already said that extroversion is symbolized by the element Fire and now, confusingly, by Cardinal signs. Indeed one of the Cardinals is a Water sign which we have correlated with introversion. If, however, we regard the elements as representing the normal state while the modes or quadruplicities indicate change of state, stress or activity this difficulty is resolved. This decision is not arbitrary. It logically follows from the fact that signs of the same element are in trine aspect with each other indicating ease or rest, while the modes are in opposition or in square with each other indicating activity and stress.

We can now re-arrange our signs in the following table:

			Cardinal Extrovert	Fixed Neutral	Mutable Introvert
Fire:	Extrovert	+	Aries	Leo	Sagittarius
Air:	Neutral	+	Libra	Aquarius	Gemini
Earth:	Neutral	-	Capricorn	Taurus	Virgo
Water:	Introvert	-	Cancer	Scorpio	Pisces

From the above it appears that the sign Aries is extrovert on both counts and Pisces introvert on both counts. The rest occupy positions in between. Extroversion-introversion does not, however, depend solely on the signs. The planets also play their part here. Prominence of Sun, Mars, Jupiter and Uranus tends towards extroversion, of Moon, Venus, Saturn and Neptune towards introversion.

The above are very broad characterisations and need to be taken with caution. Life is not like that and cannot be so neatly boxed and labelled. But such characteristics may nevertheless serve as working

The Elements

hypotheses to be verified with actual experience. We are, after all, not dealing with a fact-finding machine, but with a qualitative, suggestive conceptual framework. While the structure is coherent and logical the symbolism is suggestive and open-ended. We are given a direction in terms of meaning but no limit to how far we may travel in that direction, and no limit to the levels of meaning within the categories qualifying the direction indicated. Only actual facts of experience will determine how far we should go, on what level we must look, and what precise meaning is relevant.

With the above *caveat* in mind consider the following analogies:

Cardinal: Exterior. Visible. Palpable. The physical body.
Fixed: Central, links soma & psyche. Psycho-physical temperament.
Mutable: Interior. Invisible. Impalpable. The mind.

In embryology:
- Cardinal - The Mesoderm
- Fixed - The Entoderm
- Mutable - The Ectoderm

In physical typology:
- Cardinal - Mesomorph (Athletic)
- Fixed - Endomorph (Pyknic)
- Mutable - Ectomorph (Leptosome)

In Dr. William Sheldon's well-known temperament classification (see his 'The Varieties of Temperament', Harper & Row, New York) there are three main temperamental groups - Somatotonia, Viscerotonia and Cerebrotonia. For those not acquainted with Sheldon the following is a rough guide:

Somatotonia: Adventurous, assertive, energetic, dominating, bold, commanding, pushing, takes risks, ruthless, loud manner, gambles, drink makes him aggressive, quick reactions, seeks action when in difficulties, courageous, power-seeking.

Viscerotonia: Slow reactions, loves comfort and food, polite, relaxed, amiable, needs to be with people, needs affection, tolerant, easy going, family minded, gregarious, emotional.

Cerebrotonia: Uptight, rapid reactions but generally restrained and held in. Likes to be alone, rather secretive, unemotional, inhibited in public, dislikes crowds, sensitive to pain, quiet manner, needs to be alone when in difficulties, dislikes noise, can be unpredictable.

Translated into the language of astrology the above temperamental characteristics appear as follows:

Somatotonia: Aries, Leo, Scorpio, Sagittarius
(Sun, Jupiter, Mars)
Viscerotonia: Taurus, Cancer, Libra, Pisces
(Moon, Venus, Neptune)
Cerebrotonia: Gemini, Virgo, Capricorn, Aquarius
(Mercury, Saturn, Uranus)

The Somatotonic could be said to be 'muscle-oriented' or physical, the Viscerotonic 'gut-oriented' or emotional, the Cerebrotonic 'nerve-oriented' or mental. It will be seen that the Somatotonic correlates with three Fire signs and a Mars-ruled Water sign, the Viscerotonic with one Earth sign, one Air sign and two Water signs, the Cerebrotonic with two Air signs and two Earth signs. It will also be remarked that this three-fold division necessarily differs somewhat from the four-fold division of the elements. Such distinctions are important and serve to remind us that we are not dealing with rigid, water-tight categories but with multi-valent symbols employed as vehicles for concepts. Only the 'actual' will determine which interpretation of the 'potential' is relevant.

A further classification is that of Kretschmer[4] ('Physique and Character') who divides people into 'schizoid' and 'cycloid' types. The 'schizothyme' tends to be nervous rather than emotional, sometimes rather 'sharp', sometimes 'flat', occasionally 'brittle' or 'jagged'. The 'schizothyme' should not be confused with schizophrenic and merely refers to a type not a mental illness. The 'cyclothyme', on the other hand, is 'rounded', expansive, emotional rather than nervous and while schizothyme tends to sudden switches of temper the cyclothyme is more likely to be the subject of deep swings of mood from optimism and over-confidence to pessimism and depression and vice-versa. Significant planets: Schizothyme -

Mercury, Mars, Saturn, Uranus, Pluto. Cyclothyme - Sun, Moon, Venus, Jupiter, Neptune.

Planetary occupation of signs, elements or quadruplicities will tend to emphasize certain temperamental or psychological qualities. There are many methods of estimating the emphasis or lack of it perhaps the most used being that of adopting a 'points system'. But we cannot give the same value to the planet Pluto, for instance, as we can to the sun or moon, nor can we omit the Ascendant to which probably greater weight should be given than to any other factor. There is no fool-proof assignment of points but we suggest the following: Ascendant 13, Sun 7, Moon 7, Mercury 4, Venus 4, Mars 4, Jupiter 3, Saturn 3, Uranus 2, Neptune 2, Pluto 1 - total 50. Why, one might ask, so much to the Ascendant and nothing to the Midheaven. The latter is our focal point for our aims and ideals, for inner experience, it is private and not observable by others. It is through the former, the Ascendant, that we see others and they see us, for the Ascendant relates to our sensory-motor equipment which makes all communication with our environment and with others possible.

Let us take as an example the horoscope of the artist Pablo Picasso (born 25 October 1881, Malaga, 23.15 hours LMT, birth certificate). Our value table looks like this:

	Cardinal		Fixed		Mutable		Tot.
Fire	Aries	0	Leo	13	Sagittarius	7	20
Air	Libra	4	Aquarius	0	Gemini	0	4
Earth	Capricorn	0	Taurus	9	Virgo	2	11
Water	Cancer	4	Scorpio	11	Pisces	0	15
Total		8		33		9	50

Here, without looking further into the horoscope, we have a rough and ready basic picture. What does it show us? A predominance of Fire and Water is suggestive of an artistic temperament but stabilized by the accentuation on Fixed signs. Fire and Water incline to intuitive, instinctive behaviour with sometimes a proclivity to swing from one pole to the other. There is a surgency of temperament typical of the cyclothyme and if we add up the cyclothyme signs (Taurus, Cancer, Leo, Libra, Sagittarius, Pisces) the total comes to 37, i.e. 74%. On Sheldon's classification Picasso comes out as

Somatotonic 31 points, Viscerotonic 17, Cerebrotonic 2. How near the truth this is is questionable, but surely not too far removed from it. He was certainly a very vigorous man.

It is against such general backcloths that particular complexes, strains and stresses have to be seen and accounted for. A danger for the unwary is the idea that such a system could tell the enquirer whether the subject *actually is* extrovert, somatotonic or cyclothyme. It will not. All it can do is to indicate a potentiality which one subject may fulfil and another may not. The horoscope is not the individual person; it is merely a symbolic diagram of the qualities inherent in a certain moment in time at a certain spatial latitude and is applicable to any event whatever occurring at that time and place. The individual human being is linked to his whole world by participating with it in this moment. As Jung tells us, whatever is born or done at a certain moment in time has the character of that moment of time. In every case the individual himself and his personal experience must be taken into account and set against the potential pattern presented by the horoscope. From such a comparison much can be learned. Without it judgment is merely a potential judgment, not valueless it is true, but it should be recognized for what it is. If, for instance, a horoscope indicates that its subject is potentially extrovert but he turns out to be obviously nothing of the sort then one must look at what has inhibited the development of such a potential, either in his personal history, upbringing, etc., or by considering the horoscope of those with whom he has been in close contact, e.g., parents, siblings, guardians and so on. If, for example, his father's Saturn is conjunct, or in difficult aspect with, the subject's Sun, Moon or Ascendant this could well prove an indication of the cause of the inhibition.

V. WHOLES, HEMISPHERES AND QUADRANTS

Die Welt, die halt dich nicht, du selber bist die Welt,
Die dich, in dir, mit dir, so stark gefangen hat.[1]

(Angelus Silesius)

There is a sense in which a whole is merely the sum of its parts, and a sense in which it is more than a sum of its parts. A lump of sugar in a heap of lumps of sugar is a part of the whole, and the whole in this case is merely the sum of its lumps or parts. The relationship between part and whole is a purely mechanical one and they are not organically or necessarily connected, the one with the other. It is not so, however, with *organic* relationships, i.e., between an organism and its members. An arm is a part of the body but without the whole, the body, the part cannot exist as a living member, and without the part the whole is not a whole. The limb is only as it is when in relation to other parts and to the whole. It is in this organic sense that wholes and parts are regarded here.

Many years ago Jakob von Uexküll[2] ('Theoretische Biologie') and ('Umwelt and Innenwelt der Tiere') described the relationship between organic wholes seen as parts of larger wholes. He pointed out that different organisms lived in different immediate environmental situations ('Umwelten') due to their differing sensory-motor equipment, peripheral organs, structure, and quality of integument, e.g., skin, scales, carapace, fur, etc. The world of a dog, for instance, is very different from that of a mosquito, a snake, a beetle or a bird.[3] The interface between the individual world of the organism and the surrounding milieu (Unwelt) of its personal environment acted not only as a barrier and more significantly as a means of communication; there was a sort of functional circulation (Funktionskreis) between the two wholes. The outer world is not only different for each species but is received differently, assimilated differently and acted upon differently. The outer world's integrity or identity stops at the interface between the two worlds as does that of the individual. If it invades the organism, e.g., assimilated as food or poison or suffered as injury it immediately loses its own identity to that extent, as also does that of the organism. The invasion may result in a rise of temperature, a change in digestion, or an instinctive reaction within the organism. In this interchange the two worlds are seen to be in symbiotic relationship within a third world embracing both. This diversion into biology illustrates the relationship between wholes and parts and between wholes and other wholes which we have to consider when comparing one horoscope with another.

Astrology deals with wholes. Anything which can be described as an autonomous or semi-autonomous whole, whether it be a simple cell or a complicated organism such as the human body, can be related to a pattern of quality and potential development symbolized by a horoscope. Within a whole astrology relates the various parts each to each, and each to the whole itself. It also relates a whole to any larger whole such as the physical environment, the social milieu or group of which the whole forms a part. Each whole, indeed, may be seen from two viewpoints. Firstly that in which the human being is a whole integrating many parts, secondly that in which the individual, though a whole, is yet part of a greater whole.

In the accompanying diagram the intermediate circle represents the horoscope. The smallest circle stands for the subjective view of the world. The individual sees it as part of him, to do with as he wants. It is essentially a self-centred view. The largest circle stands for the outer world, the world of which the individual is a part and to which he has to adjust. In the diagram 'A' tries to control 'B' but finds he must adjust to 'C'.

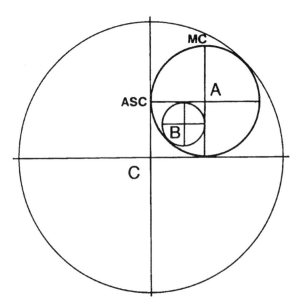

Figure 11 - Parts and Wholes, 'Worlds within Worlds'

The signs and houses divide the circle into twelve, but hemispheres and quadrants also have their related meanings. Our first example concerns the houses. Those below the Horizon relate to the subconscious, those above to the conscious, the Horizon representing the threshold between them. The former concerns impulse, instinct and innate capabilities, the latter relates to aspiration and conscious purpose.

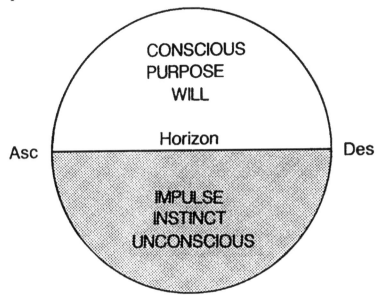

Figure 12

The houses generally, bring the subconscious forces of the sub-horizon and the unconscious forces of the zodiacal signs to the surface and confront them with the environment and the pressures of day to day life. The houses may also relate to spheres of interest indicating a mental preference in the general interaction between instinctive urges and environmental constraints. At another level the houses relate to the tangible physical body while the signs, at a deeper level, indicate congenital or hereditary predispositions affecting the body. If the signs represent a bodily diathesis or tendency to certain kinds of organic trouble or systemic dysfunction, the houses relate to the possibility of the actual materialization of disease, malfunction or accident, and they indicate the direction, the part of the organism in which such malfunction or accident or injury is most likely to occur. House aetiology is immediate resulting from the body's contact with environment - accident, injury, operation, toxins. Sign aetiology is cumulative over a period, often the result of a congenital predisposition. To take one instance - the sign Libra may relate to a constitutional diathesis involving among other things the possibility of kidney trouble. If the seventh house (associated with Libra, the seventh sign) is also emphasized then the possibility is increased. The late president John F. Kennedy suffered from adrenal trouble and had to have regular injections to keep him going. The adrenal glands relate to the Aries-Libra polarity being situated on the kidneys while their function relates to Mars. Kennedy's Ascendant was in Libra, and Mars, the significator of his seventh house (Aries being on the cusp) was placed in that house in his chart.

The division of the circle into quadrants presents us with another progression of meaning. Reading anti-clockwise the first quadrant indicates a gradual opening up from isolation, independence and self-sufficiency. The second suggests a first step in concert with others, the family circle and close relationships. The third expands contact to communities and finally the fourth reaches out to detached associations. Since, however, such associations are in the self-centred hemisphere the co-operation is largely of individuals loosely brought together by similar self-interests and while there may be mutual advantage for all self-interest is an important factor. Note that the first two quadrants being below the horizon are subconscious or instinctive associations or non-associations while the last two quadrants above the horizon are conscious associations. Finally the twelve houses and signs present us with an anti-clockwise progression from simplicity to increasing complexity.

Wholes Hemispheres & Quadrants

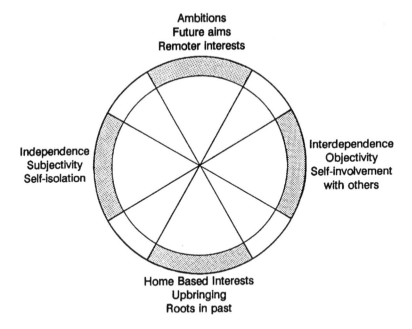

Figure 13

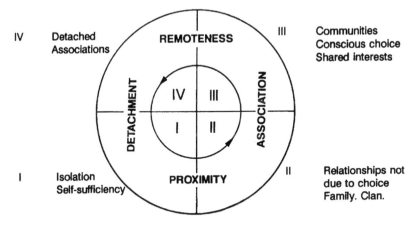

Figure 14

I and IV - Detachment II and III Association
I and II Proximity III and IV Remoteness

VI. THE SIGNS OF THE ZODIAC

'Inasmuch as the soul bears within itself the idea of the zodiac, or rather of its centre, it also feels which planet stands at which time under which degree of the zodiac....'

(Kepler: 'Harmonices Mundi')[1]

Kepler's claim that the soul bore within itself the idea of the zodiac[†] was not original. The idea goes back some two thousand years before Kepler's day to the Pythagorean physician Alcmaeon of Croton a generation before Hippocrates. A claim of such antiquity and persistence should not be dismissed out of hand without enquiry however absurd and however out of character with modern theory. It could be that something useful might be learnt.

We have encountered the three modes or qualities, the four elements and the twelve houses. Now we come to the twelve signs. Each sign has an associated planet. Some signs have two. The planets operate within the signs as different propensities coloured by the character of the signs they happen to occupy. They are then brought to the surface as it were by the houses which the rotation of the earth assigns to them. The houses rotate once in 24 hours. The sun moves round the twelve signs once in twelve months, the moon once in four weeks and the other planets at various speeds. Jupiter takes approximately 12 years, Saturn 30 years, Uranus 84 years, Neptune 164 years and Pluto 248 years. It is one of the oddities of the solar system, and there are many, that 84 + 164 = 248, i.e., Uranus + Neptune = Pluto, and that Uranus x 2 = Neptune.

The signs are not the same as the constellations of the same name. The constellations are real. They can be seen through a telescope. The signs are ideal - mental concepts like the houses. The constellations are of variable extent but the signs are all 30° sectors of the ecliptic. The departure point of the constellations is disputable. The departure point of the signs is universally the First Point of Aries (0° Aries) where the ecliptic and equator intersect at the Spring Equinox. This point is important to both astronomy and

---

[†] 'Man - a mind tied to a body - is only able to exist if this same body is an image of the universe, and if the limited portions of matter to which he has access are - in some of them - images of the universe.' (Simone Weil: 'The Notebooks').

astrology. It is a fixed reference point for calculation accepted by all. The irony is that the 'real' constellations have no generally accepted reference point while the 'ideal' signs do. At one time the signs and constellations coincided but owing to the precession of the equinoxes they have moved apart, the First Point of Aries now being in the constellation Pisces. It is with the signs not the constellations that we have to do here. The signs are to be interpreted mentally, emotionally or physically - the physical aspect relating not only to the environment, the social milieu but to the body itself, both structurally and functionally.

ARIES: Associated planets Mars and Pluto. Cardinal. Fire. Positive. Extrovert. Schizothyme. Somatotonic.

People with Ascendant, Sun or Moon, or a plethora of planets in this sign tend to regard their environment as an immediate personal challenge. There is an urge to direct attack and immediate manipulation of circumstances to their own advantage. The sign tends to egotistical, aggressive, hasty, excitable and pushing behaviour. Instincts and emotions are quick. People with this sign heavily emphasized may push themselves forward regardless of others. They have self-confidence and independence and are inclined to be rash and impetuous. They take things at face value, act before they think and go head first at things. If they meet opposition, and their nature normally invites it, they are inclined to ride roughshod over it. Quick to anger, they nevertheless rarely harbour animosity for long. They tend to be very active and like to start new projects and get things moving, though persistence is not common and the urge to move on to something else is paramount. Demanding, impatient and sometimes brusque, while they may be inconsiderate and cuttingly derogatory of anything they do not agree with they have the virtue of openness and directness, usually saying straight outright what they think. More than usually egocentric, they take a very decided and personal view. Quick to decision, sharp in action, they are impervious to advice or influence from others, and go their own way. Their minds are quick and intuitive rather than rational. They either catch on to the point at once or completely miss it. Thinking tends to be geared to action and is devoted to producing immediate results. Thought for itself is alien.

No one is one hundred per cent Aries so the above picture, as with other signs, has to be considered in company with other factors in the horoscope. Indeed if the Ascendant is in another sign the whole picture may be radically altered.

Somatic correlations: The head and face. The nose. Head injuries. Brain damage. Concussion. Cerebral meningitis. Migraine, especially when planets in Aries are in square with planets in Cancer. The function of the adrenal glands, though anatomically these relate to the opposite sign Libra. Sign correlations relate to congenital or hereditary predispositions, house correlations to accident, injury, operation or harm caused by interaction with environment. Mars in Aries might signify injury through natural impetuosity while Mars in the first house might suggest a cut to the head.

LIBRA: Associated planet Venus. Cardinal. Air. Positive. Cyclothyme. Viscerotonic. Extrovert.

Libra stands opposed to Aries in the zodiac, balances it and provides its complement in the same way as their related houses, the Seventh and the First. If Libra is seen as thesis, then Aries is antithesis and vice-versa, the two coming together in the dialectic as synthesis. In the same way that opposite houses balance each other, complement each other, then so do the signs. It follows then that a sign should never be regarded in isolation but also in relation with its opposite. The sign emphasized by planetary occupancy, or by the exigencies of particular circumstances, is taken as thesis - affirmation, its opposite sign seen as antithesis - negation. Libra is definitely *not* Aries, but it is the other face of the coin Aries-Libra and, in a sense, contains Aries within it, and, of course, vice-versa.

Libra suggests a balanced view of the world and of one's situation in it. There is little urge, in contrast to Aries, to plunge straight into experience without first weighing up the situation and making a conscious choice. Consideration is a Libra word (Lat. sidus, sideris - a star, i.e., thinking with the stars). Deliberation is an even more obvious Libra word. Where Aries is uncomplicated and single-minded there is a sort of duality about Libra. Equable and equality are other Libra words, achieving an even balance between alternatives, contrasting with the singularity and inequality of Aries. Libra people tend to be even-tempered and sociable. They usually need others or an audience being uncomfortable on their own, needing the response, appreciation and 'feed-back' that Aries ignores. Feeling and reason rather than impulse are the springs of action. The

Libra-type woos rather than rapes and tends to get more enduring results. Libra people seek to work in partnership, to co-operate with others. More than any other sign-type Librans need their complement. The Greek word for Libra (Zygon) means yoke or union and is connected with the verb Zygein - to yoke together, to bring under the yoke, to tame, to unite, and the Libra-type tends to resolve opposing forces bringing them together in harmony - the harmony in contrariety of Heraclitus. Meeting opposition it estimates its strength, dispassionately reasons with it, comes to terms with it, disarms it or tames it. Alternatively it may get locked, so to speak, in a continued dialogue, a protracted struggle, for the resolution of opposing forces is not always achievable. If Aries is the sign of challenge Libra is the sign in which challenge is taken up and the battle joined, for opposition is just as much a part of Libra as is complement and Libra as the other face of Aries contains a bit of Aries within it. One could say that within Libra there is a latent Aries - not necessarily an Aries 'fighting to get out', but all the same an Aries held in abeyance, or 'projected' onto 'the other'. The same goes for any pair of sign opposites. Each overt sign contains the germ of its covert opposite which may, on occasion, come to the surface and appear to take over. Indeed many military men and generals have been born with Libra prominent. It would appear that in the main the impetuous, impulsive, excitable Aries does not suit generalship. A balanced view of opposing forces as represented by Libra is better suited to such a career, whereas the 'gung-ho' foolhardiness of Aries might find itself better employed in a parachute regiment, commando group or mercenary soldier.

In Libra association with others is paralleled by a facility for association of ideas. It is an Air sign and unlike Aries thinking is important to it, but its inherent duality may lead to equivocation, another Libran word. Its attempt to achieve a balance between two sides is often realized in a talent for comparative evaluation achieving perhaps manifestation as art experts and dealers, valuers, marriage guidance counsellors, umpires and judges. Impartiality and dispassionate assessment are prominent qualities. Equity, equality, judgment, a keen sense of fair-play, justice and reciprocity are all Libran principles. The Aries-Libra polarity is sometimes symbolized in the statues of justice seen at law-courts where justice herself holds in her right hand a sword (Aries) and in her left a balance (Libra).

THE BALANCE OF THE ZODIAC

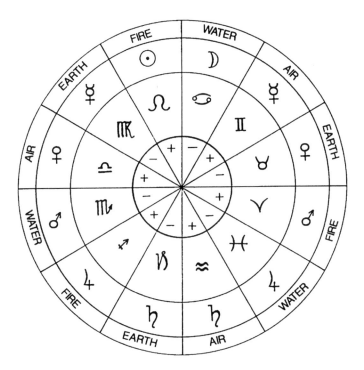

Figure 15 - Here we see the zodiac turned round so that the two major factors, the Sun and Moon, are at the top of the circle. This illustrates the subtle balance of the whole chart. In the upper sixth we have the factors of light and heat (Sun and Moon) balanced in the lower sixth by those of darkness and cold (Saturn). In the upper third we have the personal factors, Sun, Moon and Mercury, balanced in the lower third by the impersonal Jupiter and Saturn. In the left hand sixth we have the interpersonal planets Venus and Mars balanced on the right hand by their opposites, Mars and Venus, also Mercury and Jupiter on the right are balanced by Mercury and Jupiter on the left. The left-hand hemisphere exactly balances the right hand in similarity and relates to the Equinoxes when day equals night. The upper hemisphere opposes the lower and relates to the Solstices when day and night reciprocally complement each other.

Libran people do not try to dominate their social milieu as Aries tends to do nor do they attempt to change their wider environment to their advantage; they adjust to it. But if it is threatened or despoiled by others they will fight to maintain its integrity. For most of the time, however, Libra sits in that most difficult and painful of positions - astride the fence.

Somatic correlations: The waist. The lumbar region. Umbilicus. Kidneys. Adrenal glands (though their function relates to Aries). Renal circulation. Libra has reference to the skin as organ of sensation, secretion and excretion (the skin as protective integument and the nails relate to Capricorn). The idea of balance is inherent in Libra. Physiologically the references are to osmosis, the maintenance of the acid-base balance, plasma balance, blood sugar balance and the regulation of temperature between body and environment. Kidney disease. Diabetes especially where the moon is also involved (insulin secretion in the pancreas comes under the moon). Pyelitis. Glomerulonephritis. Renal calculus. Oedema. Disturbances of fluid balance. Malfunction of sweat glands. Skin troubles. Dermatitis. Eczema.

Aries - Libra: This polarity appears more susceptible than others to skin trouble, Aries to burn and blister, Libra to dermatitis whether due to external irritants or to nervous trouble. It also seems to be more liable to boils in youth and blotchiness in later life. Aries (and also Leo) sometimes inclines to freckles. Libra seems to be involved more frequently than other signs in diabetic conditions; here the renal threshold, i.e., the level of blood sugar is critical. Moreover the adrenals are important here since adrenalin affects the blood sugar level and the hormone from the adrenal cortex opposes the action of insulin. In all the above it should be emphasized that Aries and Libra are not bound to suffer any of the diseases or dysfunctions listed. It is simply that they are perhaps more likely to occur with this polarity than with others. There is a tendency which may or may not materialize. As always we are dealing with potentialities not actualities. Again the difference between congenital tendency (sign) and accidental or environmental occurrence (house) should be borne in mind.

TAURUS: Associated planet Venus. Fixed. Earth. Negative. Introvert. Viscerotonic.

Where Aries attacks and gives out, Taurus resists and takes in. The Taurus type has a desire for security as do all Earth types, though they are often the least in need of it. The innate caution of the sign demands a firm foundation for everything and it is continually trying to build up its by no means flimsy defences. Taurus people see their world as stable and down-to-earth but nevertheless in need of further construction. They see their environment as potential material for support and sustenance and attempt, if they cannot take it in, to build out of it a firm foundation for their own benefit and protection. Needs and desires may be basic and elemental but nevertheless strong and enduring. Rather fixed in his ideas the Taurus type needs very firm ground before he is convinced. Common sense and 'no nonsense' are apt phrases here. Slow to act and slow to anger the Taurus type expresses himself in a quiet, steady, unemotional, practical way. The reliability with which he is often credited is sometimes more due to inertia than to feelings of loyalty. In contrast to Aries he is sure, firm, cautious and dogged. At the extreme he may be over easy-going or, conversely, very stubborn.

The Taurus type has a hunger for not only material things but also for affection and feeling. If it lacks affection its hunger may turn in compensation to over-eating, or to collecting and storing things. In any case Taurus people incline to hoard and collect for whatever reason. Sensual, the type generally appreciates good food and creature comforts. It has strong, enduring feelings and often a developed sense of touch and hearing together with an ear for music. Not infrequently there is considerable taste and an appreciation of art. Taurus is sometimes, but by no means always, a lusty sign:

'Min ascendaunt was Taure, and ars thereinne;
Alas, alas, that ever love was sinne.'

Chaucer's wife of Bath had both the Ascendant and Mars in the sign of Venus which is often considered a strong sexual combination.

Taurus has the reputation of imperturbability and placidity. It has great endurance, is not aggressive, and will stand a lot without retaliation. But its patience is not endless and its strong, damned up feelings may break forth into violent anger. Conservative and emotional, disliking change, it understands duty and obedience but not revolt. It is no firebrand, but when it takes its stand its obstinacy and persistence can be formidable.

Somatic correlations: Mouth. Palate. Naso-pharynx. Lower jaw. Auditory meatus, inner and middle ear. Inner nasal surfaces. Larynx. Anything that falls into the Ear, Nose and Throat field of medicine. Parotid glands. Oesophagus. Thyroid and parathyroid glands. The neck. The cerebellum. The functions of the cerebellum - synergy, the balance of muscular control. The balancing function of the semi-circular canals in the ear. Disturbances of balance. Menière's disease. Note that both Venus signs, Taurus and Libra, have to do with balance. Goitre. Myxoedema. Diphtheria. Stomatitis. Mumps. Aphthae. Gingivitis.

SCORPIO: Associated planets Mars and Pluto. Fixed. Water. Negative. Introvert. Schizothyme. Somatotonic.

Scorpio and Taurus complement each other probably more comprehensively than any other opposing pair. As with Aries and Libra we find a Mars sign opposing a Venus sign. The scorpio type has a tendency to see his environment whether material or social as something to be probed, investigated and explored in depth. There is a need for depth of experience in any field whether emotional or practical. There is often a thoroughgoing determination and a desire to see things through to the bitter end. His immediate environment is seen not, as with Taurus, as something to be savoured, ingested, accumulated or built up, but as something to be examined and if necessary torn down and got rid of, especially if it impedes personal fulfilment. Destruction, elimination and reconstruction are Scorpionic principles. A deep, intense emotional life, often concealed, for Scorpio is a secretive sign, lies at the base of action. In Scorpio the sensitivity of water is at odds with the principles of the planet Mars resulting in sensitivity to attack, wounding and sometimes vitriolic retort. Unlike the other Mars sign Aries, Scorpio is slow to attack but if assailed tend to give back more than is received. 'Nemo tends me impune lacessit' would be a fitting motto. There is often a tendency to nurse wrongs. Cutting retort and sarcasm are as Scorpionic as depth of emotion and passion. Self-expression is reserved or taciturn but nevertheless forceful in a penetrating way. Here the spontaneous aggressiveness of Aries is replaced, at the extreme, by a sort of cold fury and a determination to overcome opposition even at the risk of self-destruction. The self-security of Taurus is balanced here by self-sacrifice or even self-immolation. Such extremes are, of course, rare, but the latent potentiality remains. The Taurus-Scorpio polarity illustrates symbolically the balance and contrast between feeling and sensuality on the one hand and emotion and passion on the other, between taking in (Taurus) and giving out (Scorpio). Scorpio as a Water sign senses instinctively rather than reasons, and when it does reason its logic is considerably influenced by emotion. Desires being strong and generally held under firm control there is a great potentiality for action but also a tendency for emotions to get 'bottled up'. This damning up of feeling (Taurus) and emotion (Scorpio) is typical, for both signs are 'negative' and 'fixed'.

Of all the twelve signs Taurus and Scorpio are those most associated with sex, though, of course, sex is common to all. Taurus (Venus) represents the female aspect in its inherent receptivity, sensuality and feeling; Scorpio (Mars) stands for the male aspect, ejaculatory and passionate. In the dialectic the two opposing sides fuse together in the sexual act - the synthesis. In our discussion of the houses we remarked that the eighth house corresponding to the eighth sign Scorpio was known to the Greeks as the house of death (Thanatos) and that sex was a form of death (Eros - Thanatos).[2]

This association of Scorpio with death has another side. The Scorpion is sometimes the Serpent or Dragon, but also may be the Eagle, Vulture or even the Phoenix. Deconstruction may be followed by reconstruction, regeneration and a new life. The Eagle soars above the ruin, the Vulture descends upon the carrion, the Phoenix rises from the ashes. Ideas of death and re-birth even of re-incarnation are Scorpionic. The Scorpion stings itself with its tail; the Phoenix takes on new life.

Somatic correlations: Organs of excretion and generation. Colon. Rectum. Anus. Bladder. Urethra. Ureters. Prostate. Sex organs. Sacrum. Coccyx. The pelvis and pelvic organs generally. The excretion of waste matter. Ejaculation. Colitis. Diverticulitis. Anal fistula. Haemorrhoids. Hirschspring's disease. Dysfunction of sex organs. Venereal disease. Orchitis. Hydrocele. Bladder and prostate trouble. Phagocyte action. The body's immune system. Aids.

Taurus - Scorpio: An interesting polarity. Taurus diseases and dysfunctions are reflected in Scorpio and vice-versa. Ear, nose and throat conditions have their counterparts reflected. Parotitis (mumps) may reflect on the gonads (Scorpio) the disease often being associated with orchitis or swelling of the testicles. The venereal disease, syphilis, may result in the nose being affected. Sexual changes in puberty in boys are reflected in the breaking of the voice. Anatomically the two regions are homologous and complementary: gullet - colon, pharynx - rectum, mouth - anus. Ingestion is followed by excretion. In Taurus the female function - ovulation, reception and female sexual experience generally balance and complement the male functions, sperm formation, penetration and ejaculation in Scorpio. Oral sex, cunnilingus and fellatio is also accommodated in this polarity.

The thyroid gland correlates anatomically with Taurus and its underfunction - goitre, myxoedema, slowing of the metabolic rate - fits in well with the traditional picture of Taurus as thick-necked, relatively rather slow and ponderous. Hyperthyroidism or thyrotoxicosis, however, implying a raised metabolic rate, tachycardia (rapid heart beat) and exophthalmos (protrusion of the eyeball) correlates with the Fire sign Leo in square with Taurus. The Sun (traditionally associated with Leo) may symbolize both the heart and the eyes. The parathyroids and calcium metabolism also relate to Taurus their dysfunction producing insufficiency of calcium in the blood and hence tetany, which implicates the other sign in square to Taurus - Aquarius, with its associated planets Saturn (contraction, rigidity) and Uranus (spasm).

While we have been emphasizing the importance of polarity and harmony in contrariety it will be seen from the above that the square aspect (90°) may also play a part as well as the opposition, thyrotoxicosis being just one instance. Similarly the teeth which relate functionally to Aries may also structurally come under Capricorn in square to Aries.

GEMINI: Associated planet Mercury. Mutable. Air. Positive. Extrovert. Schizothyme. Cerebrotonic.

In the progression round the zodiacal circle Aries represents action, Taurus feeling and Gemini thought. Gemini is what one calls 'mercurial' - nervously alive, with a changeable vitality. There is much intellectual activity and physical restlessness. Mental dexterity, cleverness and versatility are matched by manual dexterity and limb flexibility. Mental reactions are rapid with often a quick wit and voluble speech. The sign does not necessarily suggest mental versatility and rapidity of thought at a high sophisticated or intellectual level but it does appear to correlate with facility or articulation of both mind and body, the latter often being as supple as the mind is flexible. The fast-talking con-man, the market salesman or the acrobat are just as Geminian as the journalist, broadcaster or teacher.

Gemini types tend to see their environment in terms of communication and exchange, either mentally or physically. They tend to spend much of their time communicating and exchanging ideas, picking up and passing on information, moving restlessly from place to place. Curiosity is usually strong. They want above all to know, even if it is only trivia, and knowledge is important for its own sake - 'a snapper-up of unconsidered trifles'. Geminians know all the answers, or think they do. They are rational rather than intuitive (Aries) or instinctive (Taurus) and discussion, speaking, writing, enquiring, explaining play a large part in day to day existence. There is usually a facility for learning or picking up things quickly. Gemini relates to mental precocity, to innate mental capacity, and to such disciplines as follow from it such as logic, mathematics and music. There is often a flexibility and sensitivity of hand movement, a dexterity which is of use in any operation such as piano and violin playing, rapid type-writing, precise and deft manipulation of tools and instruments of all kinds. The nervousness is sometimes manifest in fidgeting with the fingers or gesticulating. In youth nervousness may lead to nail-biting. There is often a preference for moving about while talking.

The Gemini type is nervously alive, ill-at-ease with emotion and does not understand intuition. Everything must have a rational explanation. Discussion, argument, logic-chopping and pedantry all form part of the Geminian stock-in-trade. The type often finds it easy to take on more than one thing at a time. The duality of the

Twins is evident in the ability to jump mentally from one subject to another and back again with an agility which is often the envy of others.

Somatic correlations: The cerebral cortex. The rational part of the brain. The areas for speech, hand and limb movement in the brain. The nerves. The nervous system generally, but particularly the innervation of the means of communication - arms, hands, limbs, lungs, larynx and tongue. The nasal sinuses. The bronchi and bronchioles. The shoulders, clavicles, scapulae, upper limbs and brachial plexus. The lungs and respiratory system. Pulmonary circulation. Nerve trouble and nervous trouble, neuroses. A tendency to neuroticism. Neuralgia whether cerebral, brachial or crural. Sinusitis. Asthma. Hay fever. Bronchitis. Bronchiectasis. Pleurisy. Emphysema. Pneumokoniosis. Pneumonia. Speech defects. Lesions or disturbances of the cortex of the brain. Shoulder joint and upper arm trouble. Nervous tremor. Lung cancer.

SAGITTARIUS: Associated planet Jupiter. Mutable. Fire. Positive. Extrovert. Cyclothyme. Somatotonic.

Sagittarius complements Gemini. Both signs are quick but where Gemini (Air) is nervous and logical, Sagittarius (Fire) is impulsive and intuitive. Where Gemini is critical Sagittarius is trusting and rash. Where Gemini is witty, Sagittarius is satirical. The mind of Sagittarius reaches further, if less certainly, than that of Gemini. Less tied to the letter and with greater imagination it expands and develops beyond the bounds of an immediate rationale framework. More inclined to take chances it has greater potentiality for genuine discovery on the one hand, or for disastrous blunder on the other.

The Sagittarian tends to see the world in terms of future aims and ideals. He likes to take the long view, even if his immediate approach is an impulsive one. Freedom to expand, unfettered movement, are essential and the subject will attempt to transform, or react to environment in furtherance of this need. There is always a goal, a target to be reached. The type is inclined to be ebullient, enthusiastic and impatient. There is often great optimism and over-confidence with a tendency to extravagance and waste. An exuberant carelessness sometimes characterizes this sign. There is an inclination to overspend and overtax one's energies and, since it is a mutable, changeable sign, its vitality is subject to periods of depletion if too far extended. It is, however, a very resilient sign.

The Sagittarian mind, more imaginative than its complement Gemini, is more explorative and adventurous. Philosophy, religion, travel and exploration, foreign parts and foreign languages are frequent occupations as is the pursuit of freedom and justice as opposed to law and constraint. Although a Fire sign it is also Mutable which suggests an element of mental rather than physical substance to it. There is, then, an introversive side to this predominantly extroversive sign. In some Sagittarians everything is in the mind - the exuberance, the impetuosity is mental rather than physical, internal rather than external, and may therefore not be evident to others.

Somatic correlations: The lower limbs, especially the hip joint and thigh, ilium, ischium and femur. In the limbs this sign reflects its opposite Gemini, the hip joint as against the shoulder, the femur against the humerus. Sagittarius relates to the liver in its glycogen forming function though anatomically the liver comes under Virgo in square aspect. Note here again that the square aspect as well as the opposition may play a part. It would appear that glycogen formation and reconversion relates to the two Jupiter signs, Sagittarius and Pisces. The manufacture of the blood clotting substance fibrinogen relates to Virgo while the liver's complementary substance for clot prevention, heparin, would appear to relate to the opposite sign Pisces. The manufacture of bile in the liver relates to Virgo. The liver also manufactures a large amount of lymph, relating once again to Pisces. Disorders of hip and thigh. Congenital dislocation of hip. The sciatic nerve. Sciatica. Liver trouble. Disorders of glycogen formation. Glycosuria. Disorders of surfeit, excess, gout, obesity. Cirrhosis of liver.

Gemini - Sagittarius: This polarity appears to be more susceptible than most to nervous or respiratory trouble, asthma, hay-fever and speech defects. Another polarity almost equally involved is that of Virgo-Pisces. In Gemini-Sagittarius there is often increased flexibility of the limb joints, especially in Gemini. Flexibility can be checked by measuring the cubital angle, the extent to which the elbow can be extended. Hyperflexibility is indicated when the cubital angle exceeds 180 degrees.

Gemini, we have said, represents the upper arm. It also relates more remotely to the hand, for Gemini symbolizes the efferent nerve conduction from the motor nerve centre in the cerebral cortex through the shoulder and upper arm down to the hand. The other Mercurial sign Virgo, in square to Gemini, symbolizes the reverse flow of nervous energy, the afferent or sensory nerve conduction from hand to upper arm and sensory nerve centre in the cortex. A similar picture is presented for the lower limb by Sagittarius and Pisces. The accompanying diagram, figure 16, is illustrative.

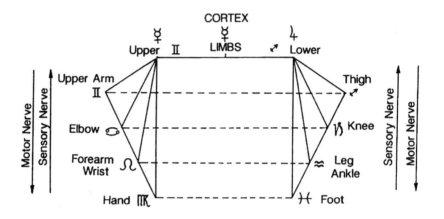

Figure 16

<u>GEMINI - SAGITTARIUS</u>

Hierarchy
Deduction - Induction
Cerebral Cortex - Limbs
Motor and Sensory Nerve Conduction

Several principles basic to astrology are symbolically represented in the diagram. Note that the positive sign Gemini is associated with the positive, motor-nerve conduction resulting in action, while the negative sign Virgo is associated with the negative, sensory-nerve conduction resulting in sensation. In an abstract sense we see here not only the idea of hierarchy, of particulars dependent on generals, of generals sustained by particulars, but also the logical methods of deduction (general → particular) and of induction (particular → general) here clearly if roughly symbolized in limb structure and movement. Note that the motor-nerve flow (downwards and outwards - head to limb) correlates with the method of deduction, the sensory-nerve flow (up and back) with induction. Note further that the pairs of opposites also carry the idea of homologues (upper arm - thigh) as indeed we have already seen in the Taurus - Scorpio polarity. Here, once again, we see the importance of the square aspect in addition to the opposition. The opposition suggests a harmony between contraries, the square a difference between similars.

CANCER: Associated with the Moon. Cardinal. Water. Negative. Introvert. Cyclothyme. Viscerotonic.

After the logical, intellectual sign Gemini comes the emotional sign Cancer. Cancer, though an introvert sign, is also cardinal and by no means inactive though its action is often more a reaction to circumstances than self-engendered. To the Cancer type the immediate environment, whether social or material, is seen as something to be enclosed, brought into a familiar local milieu if possible, to be taken in sympathetically, reflected on, digested and assimilated. The type tends to be impressionable and easily affected by circumstances, sensitive to atmosphere, the psychological 'climate' of its surroundings. The horizon is often limited, the chief focus of attention falling on the immediate milieu, on what is familiar and especially home and family which is seen as something to be enclosed, sheltered and protected, or within which it seeks its own refuge. There is an inclination to moodiness, a changeable sensitivity and a tendency to brood, but the type often presents a composed exterior with little sign of the sensitivity and emotion behind the facade. Sometimes the sensitivity of Cancer is such that a tough unyielding exterior is developed as a protection, and there is often an astonishing toughness and resilience shown once the type takes a stand. Its grip, too, can be extremely tenacious both of principle and property. Beneath the phlegmatic, sometimes poker-face front there is often great emotional force which may break out from time to time. Self-expression is quiet, welcoming. The type moves instinctively rather than rationally towards its goal, unobtrusively or indirectly perhaps, but nevertheless tenaciously. Usually there is a retentive memory and family tradition and custom mean much.

There is usually a strong protective instinct, the men tending to the paterfamilias type, the women being very maternal. With both sexes there is love of home, family and domestic life. Inheritance, heredity, family trees, inherited possessions, ancestral homes, native country together with a strong feeling of patriotism are all typical of the sign. Cancer mothers tend to like children best when they are very small, babes in arms. Pregnancy often presents little problem for them as they regard it as the most natural thing in the world. As children themselves they appear to be more than usually susceptible to parental influence and upbringing. Mars or Uranus in this sign may, however, indicate the rebel against family life.

The Cancer type tends to collect, cling and hold onto things much as the Taurus type accumulates and stores them. The over-protective or clinging parent is typical of Cancer. Shrewd and economical in spite of its emotional nature the type is very practical.

Somatic correlations: The stomach. Pancreas. Mammary glands. Lacteal and lymphatic glands. Thoracic duct. The lymphatic system generally. The elbows. The womb. Disorders of menstruation and childbirth. Diaphragm. Rib cage. Pigeon chest. Digestive juices. Hyperchlorhydria. Stomach ulcer. Mastitis. Breast cancer. There is a loose relationship between the psychological and physiological meanings of each sign. Here we see the ideas of protection and nutrition which we have already seen as connected with Cancer reflected in the thoracic cage and lymphatic system (protection), the breasts and stomach (nutrition). The womb which provides nutrition and protection for the embryo comes under Cancer from a functional point of view though anatomically it comes under Scorpio and psychologically under Taurus as the feminine complement of Scorpio. Pregnancy itself comes under Cancer, as also does the menopause.

CAPRICORN: Associated planet Saturn. Cardinal. Earth. Negative. Introvert. Schizothyme. Cerebrotonic.

Where Cancer is receptive, changeable and pliable, Capricorn is rigid, resistant, unemotional and unyielding. The Cancer-Capricorn polarity reflects the complementary aspects of content and form. The content being more important to Cancer there is a need to enclose. Form being more important to Capricorn, structure and support take precedence over protection - the skeletal framework and bone structure. The hardness of Cancer is superficial and peripheral, like the shell of a crab - a protection for a soft inside. The hardness of Capricorn is central, the spinal column or skeletal structure, the scaffolding upon which everything depends for support. In Cancer (Water) the fluid content takes the shape of the matrix; in Capricorn (Earth) the rigid framework supports, controls and determines the finished construction. This polarity of meaning is reflected in their associated symbols, the Moon and Saturn. Cancer turning back to the past in memory is yet the womb, the matrix of the future. Capricorn building the future bases its structural foundations firmly in the past, going back to tradition and well-tried methods. Capricorn takes no chances and is markedly conventional. Indeed in both signs there is an innate conservatism.

Sagittarius, as we have seen, is also concerned with future aims and goals, but there is a fundamental difference between those of Capricorn and those of Sagittarius. The element of idealism, speculation and risk present with Sagittarius is alien to the Capricorn temperament. Sagittarius sets no limits to its aims; Capricorn is more practical, knows just what it wants and sets about it in a cautious, persistent and eminently practical way to reach its goal. Capricorn on the Ascendant suggests an eminently practical view of the world and of the subject's place in it. It is seen as both a difficulty to be surmounted and as a potential firm basis for material exploitation. While negatively it may imply restriction, positively it affords the means for its eventual control. There is a strong practical drive and a need to express oneself factually, sensibly and responsibly. The manner is usually cool and controlled. There is frequently considerable ambition, a dogged determination and an urge to authoritative action and control. It shows persistence under difficulties and is so used to adverse circumstances and indeed inclined to expect them that it is not easily turned back from its goal. There is a tendency to prefer material benefits, money, position, title rather than public appreciation. This is a practical business-like combination with little nonsense about it. Obedience, must and ought are words frequently on the lips of Capricornians. As an employee the type is obedient to superiors, respects them and welcomes discipline. With this goes a strong sense of duty, application to the work in hand and a steady ambition to rise through the normal channels. Once in a position of authority himself the type becomes a firm disciplinarian demanding the same obedience and deference it once gave to its own superiors. Often courteous and polite to the opposite sex it nevertheless finds intimacy difficult. The type is often rather class and race conscious, with a defensive clannishness.

The Capricornian is sometimes a distant, severe and unbending parent finding the expression of emotion difficult while having a rather narrow, restrictive, rigid outlook and a strict code of morals tied to convention and tradition. Censorship to the Capricorn type is not the evil that it is considered to be by the Air signs Gemini, Libra and Aquarius. It thinks there is too little restriction rather than too much, except where it personally is affected. Believing in the letter of the law rather than in the spirit it takes everything literally or factually. Imagination is not its strong point. So strong is its conformism that even its ambition conforms. In the struggle up the ladder to success it will not antagonize authority for it respects it and hopes to emulate it. Command on the one hand, obedience on the other, are typical of the sign. At the extreme one has something approaching a 'master-slave' mentality.

Capricorn then, is cautious, empirical, factual, practical and sceptical of anything unorthodox. When it believes it believes in that which has the seal of tradition and convention on it. Such belief is usually unshakeable and brooks no deviation. Its scepticism is then reserved for those beyond the pale of orthodoxy. It does not take risks itself and departure from convention is a risk, though it will risk everything if it is ordered by recognized authority, for the risk of disobedience appears greater than the risk itself, and the fear of being thought afraid is worse than the fear itself. The type has many of the attributes of the ideal soldier - determination, discipline, obedience, conformism, responsibility, durability, inflexibility and the readiness, if necessary, to risk all at the behest of authority. When in command itself it becomes the martinet, exacting the same qualities from subordinates.

Somatic correlations: The skeletal framework. Bone, cartilage, ligament. The knee. The stratum corneum. The nails and teeth. The skin as protective integument - the skin as organ of sensation comes under Libra. Connective tissue generally. The spleen. The anterior pituitary gland (the posterior pituitary comes under Sagittarius). Bone disease. Calcification. Arthritis. Sclerosis. Obstruction. Acromegaly. Paget's disease. Ankylosis. Ankylosing spondylitis. Cartilage trouble. Congenital defects of skeleton.

Cancer - Capricorn: The hard outer shell of Cancer is reflected in the hard inner skeletal framework of Capricorn - the encircling rib-cage complemented by the central skeletal system upon which everything hangs. The Capricorn binge-joint, the knee, relates to the Cancer hinge-joint, the elbow, its homologue in the upper limb. The symbolism of the two signs is here seen in their function - Cancer (elbow) carrying, cradling, and Capricorn (knee) supporting, underpinning. The protective principle of Cancer is complemented by the Capricornian principle of support - stability, rigidity and structure. The rib-cage is typical of this polarity; its matter is hard bone (Capricorn) while its form is Cancerian, enclosing and protecting. It is also under this polarity that haemopoiesis comes for the production of new red cells for the blood depends chiefly on activity within the marrow of the ribs and long bones, the gastric mucosa and the spleen, all of which correlate symbolically with Cancer and Capricorn. The spleen, we remember, was considered by the ancients to be the seat of ill-humour and melancholy which again corresponds with the principle of Saturn, the ruler of Capricorn. Collagen diseases relate to this polarity. Connective tissue pertains to both Cancer and Capricorn - cartilage and bone to Capricorn, the rest to Cancer.

LEO: Associated with the Sun. Fixed. Fire. Positive. Extrovert. Cyclothyme. Somatotonic.

Following the reflective sign Cancer comes the extrovert, self-expressive sign Leo. The Leo type has wider horizons than Cancer. It tends to 'think big' and has big ideas and wide-ranging plans. Ambitious, self-confident and with great vitality it impresses itself on compeers and surroundings, seemingly without effort. There appears to be an innate feeling of superiority, whether merited or not, and its attitude to life and work appears to be that everything is, or should be, made for it - the world is its oyster. Everything centres on the individual and it is up to him to dominate it and mould it to his own purpose. The vitality associated with this sign may manifest itself in a powerful drive to organize, direct and control, or it may appear as heartiness, or as a need to show off, or where there is an underlying insecurity it may come out in the form of bluster. To the Leo type the world is a potentially splendid place - if only he could rule it. Since, however, the world is rather less splendid in fact, and individual control of even one's personal slice of it severely limited, the type is rarely satisfied, always wanting something more and sometimes, such is its pride, giving the impression that it has it when all it has is the desire. A weak Leo type is therefore at a great disadvantage for his personal pride and Weltanschauung is out of all proportion to his capabilities.

There is a tendency to extravagance and self-display with some Leos, with others a controlled but powerful 'presence'. The type as a whole inclines to seek positions of prominence whether fitted for them or not, and does not accept subordinate work readily. Indeed it does not like routine work at all, preferring to organize and delegate anything of that kind to specialists, technicians and subordinates. A position of command where it can see the whole picture at a glance and hive off detailed work to others is more in keeping with the sign. Naturally egocentric, unlike Capricorn which tends to keep a tight rein on both self and subordinates, Leo possesses a natural authority. Where Capricorn dare not relax its grip, Leo can afford to be magnanimous.

The sign has a connection with the erotic side of life, with the fundamental need to play, with the desire to give full rein to self-expression, and with the urge to take risks and spend one's vitality to the utmost. Like the Sun it relates to the 'libido' and to the creative power of the father as opposed to the protective urge of the Cancer parent, or the restrictive authority of Capricorn. The Leo type likes to gamble and take risks. Unlike the Cancer parent there is little interest in children at the cradle stage. Later, however, when the child becomes more independent, begins to play and experiment for himself, the Leo type parent comes into his own, urging the child on, joining in its games, stimulating its curiosity, widening its horizon. It does not want to protect as the Cancer parent might, but rather to stimulate, to make the child more independent, self-reliant and adventurous.

The Leo type, then, is enterprising and outward-looking, forceful and stimulating. Ready to take a chance, like Sagittarius it may well overstep itself. Self-assertive like the other Fire sign Aries, it is not so impetuous or aggressive, but more stable and dominating. In childhood the Fire signs incline to great vitality, horseplay and noise.

Somatic correlations: The heart. The Cardio-vascular system. The Aorta and Vena Cava. The pericardium. The spinal column - the thoracic vertebrae. The central circulation of the blood. The maintenance of body heat. The heart-beat and pulse. The heart as the power-centre, the engine or dynamo of the body. The fore-arm and wrist. Cardiac disease. Myocardities, pericarditis, endocarditis. Valvular disease. Dilation of the aorta, aneurysm. Coronary heart disease. Angina pectoris. Effort syndrome. Hypertension. Rheumatic heart disease. Hyperthyroidism (see under Taurus).

AQUARIUS: Associated planets Saturn and Uranus. Fixed. Air. Positive. Schizothyme. Cerebrotonic. Extrovert.

The sign Aquarius is a complicated and many-sided one. With Leo it is a 'creative' sign, but where Leo is materially creative or physically generative, Aquarius is intellectually creative or inventive. Aquarius follows Capricorn and shares with it Saturn as associated planet. But the two signs are very different. The first ten signs inclusive of Capricorn can be considered as symbolic of ten categories of normal behaviour. The last two signs, Aquarius and Pisces, are symbolic of a tendency to depart from the norm, if only marginally. This break with normality is represented by the intervention of Uranus, the other associated planet, and by Neptune in the case of Pisces. With Aquarius an element of the unusual, the original, or possibly the eccentric, however minimal, must be taken into account. For the most part, however, Aquarius is a pretty stable sign. Compared with its preceding sign Capricorn which is narrow and concentrated, Aquarius is broad and extended; it is even more broad-minded than the other Air signs. Like them it is concerned with relationships, but where Gemini emphasizes immediate practical communication, Libra two-way intercommunication and the resolution of opposites, Aquarius has a far wider range with a tendency to relate and connect remote ideas which to others might seem to bear no relationship at all.

Aquarius illustrates a type which inclines to seek meaning in its world and understanding of its laws. If it does not find them it may invent them and seek to impose them. There is a tendency to associate, to relate ideas to a pattern, to systematize and plan. Aquarius is often as abstracted in mind as in manner and there is a certain detachment and impersonality in sharp contrast to Leo. Both signs, in their different ways, have big ideas and see things as wholes rather than as parts, but whereas Leo tends to be establishment minded Aquarius is usually progressive and inclines to think ahead of its time. Originality and a revolutionary outlook, though not restricted to this sign appear to be more frequently found here than in others. With Aquarius there is a tendency to visualize and plan environment in accordance with theory rather than experience, to propose and develop advanced, radical or Utopian schemes. There is often an interest in anything that is unusual, unconventional or anachronistic whether ahead of its time, e.g., invention or radical new ideas, or an interest in the remote past, e.g., archaeology or palaeontology. The attitude to other people is democratic and egalitarian in contradistinction to the hierarchical autocracy of Leo. While Capricorn may prefer class distinctions and even segregation, Aquarius will communicate with anybody, if not in person, at least in theory, for owing to its detachment it is not a very good mixer. There is sometimes a lack of warmth and a certain aloofness distancing the Aquarian from his fellows however much he may appreciate their company. Sympathies are widespread, largely free of sectional or racial prejudice, but they may lack depth and close personal involvement. The imagination is broad and far-reaching but inclined to overlook the personal in favour of the group, or society as a whole.

There is something often rather incalculable about this sign. The subject may appear fixed or established in a certain role or way of life and suddenly without warning change course and pursue the new direction with all the appearance of having been established in it for years. Unlike Gemini, which tends to change frequently, the Aquarian switch is the more unexpected since it seemed so fixed. It is almost as though this type resented its stability and felt the need to uproot itself from time to time.

Aquarius has been described as an intellectual sign, but here reason is allied to intuition. Its capacity for rational thought is, perhaps more than with any other sign, infused with the spark of genuine originality on the one hand, or hare-brained ideas on the other. There is a need for intellectual stimulation and discussion, or just chatter, on the broadest level. It has often been considered the sign of the scientist, but this must be qualified. It does not represent the empirical scientist perhaps best illustrated by the sign Virgo. The abstract is more its field, and more akin to its principles are mathematics, theoretical science, electro-magnetism, astronomy and the science of space, fields of force, nuclear physics or cosmology - fields in which matter is either remote or is recognizable only as energy or fields of force.

The Aquarian type, unlike Capricorn, dislikes authoritarianism and detests restrictions on freedom. Sagittarius, too, is freedom loving but while Sagittarius chooses situations enabling it to have free range of movement without radically altering its environment Aquarius wants the whole system changed if it is at all restrictive or authoritarian. Utopianism is often strong but there is, however, a proclivity to doctrinaire theory, to a love of principle at the expense of common sense, and in the process of bringing about its plans for the betterment of human conditions it sometimes veers towards authoritarianism itself. Both Krishnamurti and Karl Marx had Aquarian Ascendants.

Detached in mind, abstract in intellect, sometimes a little aloof in social contact, the Aquarius type is nevertheless not unsociable. But it does not readily become intimate. Relationships are friendly but restrained resulting often in many friends and acquaintances but few that are really close. There is often a difficulty in confining sympathy to one person, or even the family, and it may extend in diffused form to people and humanity in general in stark contrast to Capricorn where charity begins at home and rarely leaves it.

Usually the sign type has little respect for convention and custom. Convention is seen as an unnecessary strait-jacket rather than, as with Capricorn, a buttress for support. Frustration in its aims may lead to crankiness. Though often progressive and revolutionary in its ideas it is frequently ineffective in practice, preferring to let its ideas remain ideals than commit itself.

Somatic correlations: The peripheral circulation in the capillaries, arterioles and venules of the tissues. The control of vascular tone. The lower leg, calf and ankle. dorsalis pedis pulse and posterior tibial pulse. Disturbances of dysfunction of peripheral circulation or central nervous system. The central nervous system. The spinal cord. The control-release mechanism of the nervous system (cf. the associated planets, Saturn - control, Uranus - excitability). the dorsalis pedis and posterior tibial pulses are important in the diagnosis of peripheral vascular disorders such as thrombo-angiitis obliterans (Buerger's disease) which involves acute pain, particularly in the calf muscles. Here the pulses, the nature of the disease and the site of the pain all evoke the symbolism of Aquarius. Leg cramps. Spastic conditions such as in upper motor neurone diseases. Direct injury to leg or ankle.

Leo - Aquarius: This polarity being concerned with the function of the cardio-vascular and central nervous systems has wider and more far-reaching ramifications than any other. We have here, as it were, the 'power axis' of the whole body with its central structure the spinal column carrying within it the neural cord and along side it the major blood vessels, the largest in the body, the aorta and vena cava. Moreover, Uranus (associated with Aquarius) relates to the sino-astrial node in the heart (Leo), which node, often known as the 'pace maker' of the heart, controls the rate of heart-beat. Those parts of the limbs associated with Aquarius - the legs and angles - are complemented in Leo by the fore-arms and wrists. These bones are particularly liable to fracture (Saturn-Uranus) - 'Colles' fractures of the lower end of the radius, and 'Pott's' fractures of the fibula. Bone and break relate symbolically to Saturn and Uranus respectively, the planets associated with Aquarius. This Leo-Aquarius axis carrying the circulatory and central nervous systems lies at right angles to the Taurus-Scorpio axis symbolizing the digestive system (Taurus - ingestion, Scorpio - excretion) completing a powerful fixed sign cross.

VIRGO: Associated planet Mercury. Mutable. Earth. Negative. Schizothyme. Cerebrotonic. Introvert.

Following Leo in the zodiac Virgo presents a striking contrast. Where Leo see things in the round and in wholes the Virgo type sees them in detail and separately. The first can't see the trees for the wood, the second can't see the wood for the trees. Where Leo is self-confident Virgo inclines to self-possession and self-conceit, especially in matters of skill and intellect. While Leo tends naturally to assume positions of command, virgo is often considered the sign of 'service', and those with the sign Virgo prominent often seek positions and careers in which they can be of service to others.

The Virgo type sees its world as something to be investigated, catalogued, analyzed or critically assessed. It looks at life in detail, even microscopically, and wants to see exactly how everything functions. Everything is noticed down to the smallest detail and precision is all important, a good basic foundation for a scientist or technician. Its world is regarded as material for the employment of practical skills and technological exploitation. The Virgo type is usually an excellent worker, reliable, skilful, quick, precise and painstaking. It is the sign of the craftsman, the precision engineer and draughtsman, the efficient secretary, computer programmer or needlewoman. Neat, orderly, clean, precise the type rarely gets things in a mess for it knows just how to manipulate things and things do not object to be kept in order, catalogued, pigeon-holed and arranged. Its understanding of people, however, is less sure and there is a tendency to treat them too as things. Social contacts tend to be kept, if possible, at arms length and on a practical no-nonsense plane, for intimacy for this type is not easy and is sometimes unwelcome.

Virgo shares its associated planet with Gemini but where Gemini represents the positive side of the intellect - rational, enquiring, theoretical, communicative, discursive, Virgo represents the negative side - empirical, testing, analyzing, sifting, discriminating, refusing to countenance anything that cannot be weighed or measured, or which has no practical application. The Virgo type often has a cool, unassuming, critical manner. There is good memory for detail and practical matters and the imagination is brought down to earth and held in tight rein. Cautious and nervous there is a tendency to worry, especially about health. Unsure of itself psychologically the type seeks a firm, practical, down to earth base. There is often a 'no nonsense' manner adopted as a protection against anything it considers, unsafe, unorthodox, unproven or irrational. There is a tendency to understatement and deflation of others but as a rule there is no underestimation of the subject's own intellect and skill and there may well be some conceit. On the other hand the type may sometimes be devastatingly self-critical.

The outlook is often rather narrow and specialized. There is also sometimes an inclination to intolerance of others, especially if they do not measure up to the subject's own precise, practical standards. The type is shrewd and unsentimental, rarely taken in by others, and the worst sin is to be taken for a fool. Fools, indeed, are not suffered gladly. A perceptive critic with a fine discrimination the type may sometimes descend to pettiness, fuss or a finicking attention to trivia. Obsessive house-cleaning, tidiness and compulsive hand-washing are Virgo traits and, to a lesser extent, those of Gemini too. Sometimes there is pedantry.

Virgo does not understand emotion but is well acquainted with 'nerves'. Although outwardly impassive, a tight rein being kept on the emotions which it fears, its nerves sometimes get the better of it and the type appears rather susceptible to psychosomatic trouble. Being a Mercurial sign the intelligence is quick, though not as quick as Gemini, tending to be more cautious and methodical. The nervousness of both signs is sometimes betrayed in fidgeting or fiddling, though with Virgo the restlessness is usually better controlled. General expression is usually cool, composed and nervously impassive. Movements are rapid, precise and nervous but well controlled, a kind of restrained restlessness. Speech tends to be quick, nervous, dry, matter of fact and deflating.

Somatic correlations: The small intestine - duodenum, jejunum and ileum. The liver and gall-bladder. The splanchnic nervous system. The coeliac or solar plexus. The portal circulation. The secretion of bile from the liver (the production and storage of glycogen in the liver comes under Jupiter and Sagittarius in square with Virgo, or more probably under Jupiter and Pisces). The further break down of food from the stomach (Cancer) and its assimilation. Peristalsis of the small intestine. The hands and fingers.

Intestinal trouble, especially of nervous origin. Nervous stress tends to be reflected in intestinal upsets, duodenal ulcers, etc. Enteritis. Ileitis. Cholecystitis. Jaundice. Intussusception. There is a link with the other mercurial sign Gemini, with the lungs and nervous system generally. Both Gemini and Virgo appear sensitive to asthmatic and respiratory complaints. Disturbances affecting fingers and hands. Nervous tremor.

PISCES[†]: Associated planets Jupiter and Neptune. Mutable. Water. Negative. Introvert. Cyclothyme. Viscerotonic.

Following the complicated mental sign Aquarius, Pisces, the last sign of the zodiac, reaches the peak of sensitivity and subtlety. This most impractical of signs opposes and complements the practical and matter-of-fact Virgo. The last two signs are especially difficult to understand, Pisces even more than Aquarius. Compared with them the preceding ten signs are relatively orthodox while the first two, Aries and Taurus, are simplicity and directness itself. These last two

---

[†] The sign Pisces is not only the domicile of Poseidon (Neptune) but also of Chaos. Anti-clockwise Pisces (Chaos) is the last sign in the zodiac; clockwise it is the first. In the Greek mythology of Hesiod the origin of the cosmos was Chaos - vast, chaotic, elusive, insubstantial and limitless. In Greek the word 'chaos' suggests gaping, open space and it is the origin of our word 'gas', again indicative of the sign Pisces.

are not notable for decision and action. Their *forte* is understanding - Aquarius intellectually, Pisces instinctively and sympathetically. The contrast with Virgo is dramatic. With Virgo we have precision, concentration on the matter in hand, caution and preoccupation with detail. With Pisces we see a tendency to carelessness in material things, difficulty in concentration and sometimes confusion and muddle. Pisces is impressionable and susceptible. While Virgo is rarely taken in by others, suffers fools with difficulty and is shrewd, careful and sparing, Pisces is frequently deceived, overtrusting and prodigal. Virgo finds it easy to say 'no'. Pisces finds it extremely difficult. If Virgo is narrow, tense, defensive and self-protective then Pisces is broad, overflowing in its sympathy and extremely vulnerable. Virgo sometimes displays a rather narrow moral attitude. Pisces is more interested in ideals than morals. Indeed, morally, it tends to permissiveness.

Just as there are two main types of Aquarian, the Saturn or stable type and the Uranian or unconventional type, there are two main types of Pisces, the Neptune type and the Jupiter type. The Neptune type tends to be sensitive, subtle, vulnerable and unconventional though the unconventionality is usually not marked, as it may be with Aquarius, being not so much a break with convention as an indifference to it. The Jupiter type is more robust, is not averse to good company, has a good sense of humour often rather surrealist, can be a bit of a blusterer (Falstaff is a good example) though not violent, and tends to go to extreme for Pisces knows no limits. The saint and the sinner, the nun and the whore are Piscean types. In business the Pisces type is usually a sorry failure or, if successful, may become a multi-millionaire, wealthy entrepreneur or financial fraudster. The Protean nature of this sign is bewildering and difficult to grasp containing extremes of poverty and wealth, idealism and deception.

The Pisces type is often absent-minded, rambling and unmethodical and there is sometimes a tendency to drift. Often vague, imprecise, secretive and withdrawn there is, nevertheless, on occasion a sort of casual, quiet good humour. Unlike its opposite Virgo, Pisces being viscerotonic does not hold itself aloof from its fellows and longs for approval if not affection. At the other extreme it may, like the anchorite in his cave, or the monk in his cell, cut himself off completely from others. Generally the type tends to be tolerant in mind and relaxed in body, with little sense of immediacy or urgency. The Pisces type is usually not very good with its hands (which relate to Virgo) and is more likely to be clumsy than otherwise. But if it is not very good at doing it is extremely sensitive and feeling. Its mind, too, knows no bounds. Routine work which Virgo tackles with efficiency Pisces considers anathema. The poet, the musician, the abstract thinker and the artist are more in its line for it is very imaginative and intuitive. If it does go in for science it is usually theoretical science or mathematics that attract, not the practical science of Virgo. Einstein had the Sun in Pisces and Pisces on his Midheaven. Virgo may provide the run of the mill scientist but for the real top-notchers where imagination is at a premium Pisces seems to crop up surprisingly frequently. Similarly with the Aries-Libra polarity it is the Libra pole that appears to relate to the top military men, the generals, not the Martial sign Aries. Polarity should never be neglected. The Pisces type is more liable than others to physical exhaustion and lassitude, but it possesses a strong inner elasticity. As with the precepts of the Tao Teh Ching it overcomes by yielding. A frontal attack is anathema the type preferring to yield, by-pass or subvert, the subject feeling his way rather than forcing it with the result that it is sometimes accused of deviousness or over-subtlety. Pisces sees its world as impermanent and insecure and unlike Virgo does not accept it as it appears, at face value. It needs to look below the surface. The everyday world of appearance is an illusion, the 'Maya' of Hindu philosophy. Einstein's theory of relativity has shown us something of what may lie behind appearance. If the world itself is not seen as insecure then the Pisces type will certainly feel itself to be insecure in it, and may tend to retreat from it into itself. Alternatively it may see the world not so much in the light of material immediacy but as full of latent possibilities, or as a field for imaginative exploration and exploitation with no limits and no legal obstructions (the Pisces entrepreneur). Generally, however, the type mistrusts the everyday world, distrusts its values, ignores or by-passes its conventions and prefers to contract out of the struggle into less competitive fields. There is often a strong social conscience with much sympathy and consideration for others regardless of colour, creed or social status. The outcast, the handicapped and the 'underdog' frequently excite sympathy from Pisces types.

Pisces individuals are often sensitive to 'atmospheres', to changes in the weather, to gases, smells, anaesthetics, drugs or hypnosis. Many appear to have a strong fear of, or revulsion for drugs. Others succumb to drug taking or alcohol. They tend to be deep sleepers and over-sensitive to pain. The type often appears more indecisive and impractical in daily life than it really is; or it may give an impression of outward efficiency or conformity which is quite at variance with its underlying nature. More than any other type it is difficult to pin down and tends to elude attempts at precise classification. The zodiacal circle which began with simplicity ends in a bewildering complexity.

Somatic correlations: The feet and toes. In Pisces there is a link with the fluid content of the tissues and the feet especially are liable to swelling from excess fluid. Inundation of tissue, extravasation, oedema, dropsy, relaxation of tissue, flaccidity and loss of muscle tone. The nervous sensitivity of Virgo is here replaced by psychic sensitivity. Sometimes there is a sort of sixth sense or paranormal perception. Clairvoyance, clairaudience, extrasensory perception, dowsing and divination are occasional manifestations and, if rare, at least more attributable to this sign than to others. Proneness to vague fears, presentiments and delusions. Susceptibility to drugs, smells, gases, intoxicants, alcohol, infection and allergies. Oversensitivity to pain and to anaesthetics, often not taking the latter well or can be easily overdosed. Sometimes there is a horror of losing consciousness. Diet is important with sometimes an emphasis on 'whole-food' or vegetarianism. Similarly there is often a predilection for holistic or alternative medicine or homeopathy.

It is possible, even probable, that liver function in its glycogen formation aspect should be ascribed to Pisces rather than to Sagittarius; in any case Jupiter is involved as significator. Psychic troubles. Chaotic conditions. Hallucination. Delusions. Mental confusion. Paralysis of the will, or of the body. Neptune, though not necessarily Pisces, is apparently often involved in cases of paralysis. Dream states. Fantastic flights of imagination. Religious rapture

Virgo - Pisces: This polarity, probably more than any others, is indicative of psychosomatic trouble. Pisces especially appears prone to ills of an unusual nature difficult to diagnose, or tends to react to normal ills in an abnormal way. Though it may more easily succumb to disease than other signs it has a latent elasticity and a surprising capacity for recovery. On the other hand it may just 'give up', resigned to its condition. Virgo tends to keep on an even keel but with Pisces it is usually all or nothing.

Appearance

Just as no one is wholly extrovert or wholly introvert so no one is one hundred per cent Capricorn or Leo. As, with Kepler, 'the mind bears within itself the idea of the zodiac', so does the body. Correlations with parts of the body have been added since the body is an extension of ourselves into our environment and is the medium through which the interchange between ourselves and our environment is achieved. In astrology the whole of the zodiac is represented in the body, just as in the mind. Character delineation rests on some signs being more emphasized than others, the emphasis depending on the Ascendant and planetary occupation. If the Ascendant, sun, moon and planets are all in one sign then we have a clear picture but this is never the case. In most instances the emphasis rests in three or four or more signs so that the picture is a composite one, the emphasis on one sign having to be balanced against the emphasis on others so that no clear cut picture of any sign characteristics shows through. Even those signs unoccupied are not negligible since they are in relationship with those occupied by aspect and, if in opposition, for instance, may act as 'not-self' to the 'self', as negation or complement or, in the case of a square aspect, as obstruction or dysfunction. The sorting out of such a complex picture is an art demanding considerable skill. Nevertheless, unless the emphasis is spread evenly round the circle, concentrations of emphasis will present us with recognizable characteristics, the Ascendant sign being the most likely to show up, followed by the sun and moon signs, or the sign containing the planet ruling the Ascendant.

A difficulty here is the location of the Ascendant since it depends on the time and place of birth and the time is often not known. However one can sometimes get a clue to it from physical appearance and mannerisms. A curious aspect of astrology is that noticeable bodily peculiarities may be indicated in the horoscope. This can be checked by anyone who knows his own chart or the horoscopes of family and friends. The major factors apart from the most important, the Ascendant, are the sun and moon; Mars and Saturn are also sometimes important. Signs and houses relate to parts of the body as follows:

Aries and First:	Head and nose.
Taurus and Second:	Ears, lower jaw and neck
Gemini and Third:	Collarbone, shoulders and upper arm.
Cancer and Fourth:	Elbows, rib-cage, breasts, stomach.
Leo and Fifth:	Fore-arms and wrists, the back.
Virgo and Sixth:	Hands and fingers.
Libra and Seventh:	Waist, navel, sometimes also breasts.
Scorpio and Eighth:	Genitalia and pelvis.
Sagittarius and Ninth:	Hips and thighs
Capricorn and Tenth:	Knees.
Aquarius and Eleventh:	Legs and ankles.
Pisces and Twelfth:	Feet and toes.

We have here confined ourselves to what is visible. Tenancy of any sign by Ascendant, Sun or Moon suggests a peculiarity or some excess or deficiency in the part of the body signified - a mole, double-jointed fingers, flat feet, a strawberry mark, broader or narrower than normal hips, birth marks of any kind, etc. Occasionally the peculiarity may be abnormal perfection - exceptional beauty, but whether it suggests perfection or imperfection it is nevertheless a departure from the norm. Tenancy of any house rather than sign by Sun, Moon, Mars or Saturn suggests that the deviation is accidental rather than congenital. In my own case I have Mars in the first house and the top of my head is covered with scars as the result of my inadvertently and repeatedly banging it over the years. I have had the opportunity of verifying this strange sort of link between planetary position and bodily marking on scores of occasions with different people and have rarely been disappointed, though not every potential materializes. However it so stretches credulity that I hesitate to include it here. However fact, despite its unpalatability, should not be heedlessly overridden by accepted theory and the matter is easily verifiable. Experientia docet. One advantage of this is that if the birth-time and thus the Ascendant is not known and there is a manifest abnormality in, say, the feet and yet nothing at all in the sign Pisces, then this could be taken as an indication that the Ascendant might well be in Pisces. Like everything in astrology, however, this is no cast iron rule. While science seeks certainties astrology merely provides us with pointers and guide lines. With this in mind a rough guide to the locating of the Ascendant in a sign is the following table of physical appearance and mannerisms associated with each sign of the zodiac. The delineations are based on people of European or 'Caucasian' origin and must therefore be modified for other races.

ARIES:
Appearance: Usually rather lean and sinewy, but muscular. Narrowish head. Strong eyebrows. Sharp eyed. Tendency to poke head forward. Prominent nose, sometimes up-tilted, more often straight and narrow. Thin cheeks, often prominent cheek-bones. Thinnish, sometimes stringy neck. Thin lips. Prominent chin. Another type is broader but compact and muscular. Skin often fair, may be freckled, liable to sun-burn. Face pale or reddish. Hair can be reddish or fair, rarely dark.

Movement and Mannerisms: Self-confident, urgent, aggressive, pushing. Energetic, rash. Peremptory. Quick, forceful driving movement. Quick, excitable reactions. Goes head first at things. Active, impulsive walk. Quick to anger. Decisive. Brusque. Intolerant.

Speech: Strong, sharp, ringing tone. Incisive, peremptory, urgent.

LIBRA:
Appearance: Tendency to slimness in youth, putting on weight in middle age. Often good looking and well-proportioned body with a certain elegance. This is usually the best looking of the signs. Fresh complexion. Sensitive skin, usually fair. Longish head with oval face, rounded chin. Regular features. Sometimes in middle age there is a tendency to bags under the eyes or blotchiness of the skin.

Movement and mannerisms: Measured. Lithe, graceful walk. Sometimes rather lazy or languid movements. Balanced. Accomplished. Finished. Friendly, sociable, welcoming. Diplomatic manner.

Speech: Even, measured, sometimes a drawl. Occasionally can be 'affected'. At other times strong, level, clear. There is little sense of urgency and words are weighed. In contrast to Aries, Libra thinks before speaking. Tactful.

TAURUS:

Appearance: Rather solid, thick set, sometimes heavy-looking. Thickish, shortish neck, though in women often long and strikingly beautiful. The usually broad body is sometimes accompanied by relatively small and neat extremities; alternatively rather large, fleshy hands. Rounded head, shortish nose, full lips. Sometimes the body is altogether less solid being well-proportioned, especially in women, but it is rarely thin.

Movement and mannerisms: Slow, deliberate, dignified. In women movements can be graceful, rounded. Quiet, determined, sometimes lazy, sometimes ponderous. Slow reactions. Warm. Friendly. Imperturbable. Steadfast.

Speech: Slow, deliberate delivery. Pleasant tone, sometimes soft, sometimes low and strong. Can be musical. Often a good singing voice.

SCORPIO:

Appearance: Strong, firm, muscular, compact. Lower limbs sometimes out of proportion, often being relatively short. Occasionally bow legs. Often a shortish thick neck and firm strong chin. Wide thin-lipped mouth. Cheekbones and eyebrows are often prominent, the eyes being deep-set and piercing. The nose is often aquiline. Broad shoulders and relatively long arms. Occasionally there is a leaner, more ascetic type with nevertheless an impression of hidden strength. There is an impression of hidden depths of emotion but of great control.

Movement and mannerisms: Dignified, purposeful, forceful yet restrained. Sometimes and rolling gait. Can sometimes seem rather menacing, or sexy.

Speech: Measured, incisive, serious, penetrating. Sometimes deep or 'gravelly'. Can be cruelly sharp-tongued but unlike Aries not 'off the cuff' but from the depths of injured emotion. In some Scorpios the voice is noticeably 'sexy' and the low voice of Scorpio women especially so.

GEMINI:

Appearance: Usually slim and flexible build, but can be broad-shouldered. Seldom muscular or fleshy. Smallish, narrow, long head with bony construction emphasized. Tendency to narrow chest, long arms and fingers. Long, narrowish, sensitive nose, sometimes rather pinched looking. Pointed chin. Face rather triangular with narrow chin and broad brow. Thin cheeks and narrow lips. Thin neck with prominent collar bones. Sharp eyed, alert look. Usually pale complexion. Often great flexibility of limb. Youthful look.

Movement and mannerisms: Quick, nervous, restless. Precocious, irreverent, variable, fizzing with ideas, quick reactions, nervous gestures, tendency to fidget or gesticulate. Fingers often in continuous movement. Can't sit still for long. Rapid, nervous drive and activity, quick witted, critical, rapid speech with tendency to switch rapidly from subject to subject. Often a good mimic. Usually prefers city life to the country. Clever. Deft with his hands. Inconstant.

Speech: Rapid, nervous, logical. Voluble, witty, critical. Tendency to switch rapidly from subject to subject. Sometimes a rather flute-like, high-pitched voice, but on occasion deep and strong. Mischievous, chatty, gossipy. Argumentative, hair-splitting. Ingenious, clever, throwing off ideas. Coruscating.

SAGITTARIUS:

Appearance: Usually well built, on the slim side, but may well put on considerable weight in middle age, but even if corpulent, more buoyant than ponderous. Long legged, flexible, muscular, springy. Keeps youthful look well into middle age.

Movement and mannerisms: Eager, forward looking. Quick, long stride. Sometimes a sort of loping gait. Sometimes a stoop. Purposeful. Enthusiastic, ebullient. Quick reactions. Tends to walk and talk. Usually needs a lot of exercise - generally walking, 'jogging' or running. Impulsive, impatient. Frank, open, optimistic, lively, jocular, exaggerative, high spirited, sometimes waggish or satirical but can be absurdly pompous. A sporting type. Prefers the run of the country to town life - shooting and hunting, especially riding.

Extravagant, generous, careless, over confident. Great vitality and elasticity. Welcomes risk. Has far reaching ideas and can be studious, even academic.

Speech: Rapid, exaggerative, amusing, lively, jocular, sometimes waggish or satirical. Tendency to use racy language or slang, on the one hand, or colourful, inflated or pompous phrases on the other.

CANCER:

Appearance: Fairly large, round head. Wide, full mouth, sometimes rather slack. Upper half of body sometimes looks too big for lower half. Relatively short legs. Shortish, pointed fingers, soft hands. Loose, slack sub-cutaneous tissue. Strong growth of hair. On occasion there is a slimmer, more supple type or, at the other extreme a type with narrower skull, angular face and aquiline nose. Pale skin. Calm eyed. Sensitive, receptive, caring.

Movement and mannerisms: Welcoming, protective, hospitable, busy, house proud, caring. Family minded, fond of children. Active yet unobtrusive. Practical in matters close to home and family. Moody, long suffering. Imaginative, good memory.

Speech: Quiet voice, often rather characterless and flat. Tendency to reminisce or gossip.

CAPRICORN:

Appearance: Angular, usually rather lean body. Bony. Large bony hands and feet. Narrowish head. Bony face. Leathery skin. Sparse hair in males; in females often an abundance of hair. Facial creases accentuated. Long deep creases at sides of mouth. Long, stringy neck, sometimes with 'Adam's apple'. Tendency to hold himself stiffly.

Movement and mannerisms: Often rather awkward, stiff and ungainly. Punctilious, often courteous and chivalrous. Purposeful, cautious but determined. Sober, practical, active, regular, disciplined, law abiding, conventional. Can be hard and unrelenting or diffident and mistrusting. A strict authoritarian himself who can be obsequious to those in authority over him. Obedient while demanding obedience. Sometimes rather distant and unapproachable. Obstinate yet polite and courteous to the opposite sex. Manners are important. Austere, frugal, parsimonious. A pessimist. Relies on fact, tradition and convention and has little imagination. Rectitude and reliability.

Speech: Flat and conventional. Sometimes taciturn, but once started difficult to stop. Can be very loquacious. Matter of fact. Dry. Deflating. A great one for reminiscences, also for facts.

LEO:
Appearance: Powerful, resilient, well-proportioned body. Large round head often with prominent eyes and a tendency to stare through people. Broad shoulders. Occasionally there is an abnormally small type of Leo with, nevertheless, an impression of weight and consequence. Face more square than oval. Broad brow, squarish chin. Large, strong mouth. Fresh complexion, sometimes reddish, sometimes freckled, with tendency to sunburn. Powerful fore-arms and hands. Average to small but well-formed nose. Usually fair to light brown hair, or reddish. Imposing appearance with sometimes a tendency to showy or luxurious dress, especially in women.

Movement and mannerisms: Dignified (all 'Fixed' signs have some degree of 'dignity'). Forceful. Imposing. Self-confident. Commanding manner. Must make his presence known. Authoritative. Intuitive. Colourful. Leo tends to show off and is sometimes pompous and vain to the point of inviting ridicule. Risk and chance play a large part in his life - gambling, games, sport, the theatre and show-business, speculation and entrepreneurship. Anything large and showy with a dash of risk tends to attract. Sometimes a bit of a womaniser or, if a woman, a man-chaser. Philoprogenitive. Creative. Likes to be top dog in anything he undertakes.

Speech: Strong, deep or rich voice. Loud, commanding tone. Colourful expression with a tendency to embellish the facts and exaggerate. Bluff. Tendency to talk big, or in general terms with little attention to detail.

AQUARIUS:

Appearance: Average build. Generally loose, relaxed bearing but can tense up from time to time under mental strain. Good muscle structure but without an impression of muscular strength. Broad head, rounded, oval face, broad cheek bones and chin. Often a pale, rather transparent skin, sometimes rather easily flushed. Hair inclines to greyness rather early in life. Hair fair or flaxen or alternatively dark or black with a slight bluish tinge. The flaxen hair occurs in those of Nordic or Scandinavian extraction.

Movement and Mannerism: Quiet, dignified carriage. Calculated, easy and relaxed movements. Sometimes an impression is given of aloofness, or of superiority over others of similar background. Rather cool and detached. Deliberate reactions, sometimes an abstracted air. Broadminded, wide interests. Ingenious, inventive, unconventional. Interested in anything very new or revolutionary, new inventions and technology, or in the very old e.e., archaeology or palaeontology. Occasionally the type gives an impression of unusualness, muted, indefinable, but nevertheless noticeable. At times there may be little eccentricities of manner, sudden, unexpected odd or bizarre gestures.

Speech: Usually rather quiet, even toned, 'cultured', rational yet at the same time imaginative and inventive. Sometimes there are eccentricities of expression, neologisms, or an odd choice of words.

VIRGO:

Appearance: Usually neat, compact, well-proportioned, firm. High brow tending to go bald at the sides - 'widow's peak'. Oval face. Often a youthful appearance. Sometimes a slimmer, more wiry type of body. Cool, observant, critical eyes that miss nothing. Thin lipped, rather small mouth. Often a 'poker face' giving nothing away. Usually good bone structure but not muscular. Wiry, capable hands with waisted fingers. Nervous though not always noticeably so since the nerves are usually kept well under control. Intelligent, adroit, skilful, critical, precise, discriminating, occasionally nit-picking or pedantic.

Movement and mannerisms: Nervously controlled movements. Quick nervous reactions, though not as quick as Gemini. Very clever with hands - craftsmanship, needle-work, machining, drawing, graphic work, carpentry, modelling, etc. Like Gemini the fingers are often in continuous movement but less noticeable and better controlled.

Speech: Matter of fact. Flat. Unemotional. Deflating. Understating. Logical. Critical. Though generally quiet and undemonstrative the voice may become sharpish or shrewish under pressure, sometimes devastatingly self-critical. Caution and underestimation. A defensive 'no-nonsense', down to earth manner of speaking. Occasionally criticism may develop into nagging.

PISCES:
Appearance: Usually average to small stature with fine bone structure and poor musculature. Resilient, supple, slack, round-shouldered. Often a rather short, thickish neck. There is also, especially in women, a very fine-boned, delicate, almost ethereal type. Again, more often in men, there is a more robust, larger, bulkier Falstaffian type. Pisces is difficult to pin down being Protean with many shapes and sizes. the Falstaffian type relates to the planet Jupiter, the ethereal type to Neptune. The eyes tend to be slightly protruding and are rather watery or dreamy, abstracted. Pisces eyes, unlike Virgo's, are not very good at noticing detail but they take in colour and aesthetic appreciation is above average. The mouth is usually full and rather loose. Rounded chin tending to become a double chin rather earlier than usual. Soft, fine hair, usually dark. Loose skin and subcutaneous tissue tending later to go into folds. The skin is often very soft and sensitive and may become lined in later life the creases deeply furrowing the face. Alternatively, such is the 'all or nothing' aspect of Pisces, remaining smooth and unlined, showing hardly any aging at all.

VII. THE GEOMETRY OF MEANING

We have been dealing with the signs as if the categories of meaning so illustrated were immutable and indisputable. They are, on the contrary, just those aspects of astrology most in dispute. Indeed, some astrologers have attempted to operate without them. The sun, moon and planets are phenomena present for all to see. The Meridian and Horizon are verifiable by means of the earth's rotation. No problem there. But what of the signs? Where is the evidence? They are not, like the constellations, visible to the eye. They cannot be said to 'exist'. Their only link with reality is their starting point, the First Point of Aries, the Spring Equinox, an indisputable reference point for both astronomy and astrology. It would appear that they are mere projections of the human mind or, as Alcmaeon of Croton and Johannes Kepler maintained, intimately if subconsciously related to the mind itself. Does the mind categorise meaning in this twelve-fold fashion? That it *appears* to think in *a* dodecanate manner is supported by Kant's twelve *a priori* categories and judgments, by Aristotle's three propositions of the syllogism multiplied by the four types of syllogism and by numerous other examples some of which have already been mentioned. Can, then, the signs by *deduced* from the pattern or 'Gestalt' of the twelve-fold chart? We suggest that broadly and vaguely, as befits universals, they can. Our instrument for such deduction is the geometrical angle or 'aspect'.

Aspects derive from the Pythagorean idea of multiplicity developing out of unity. The origin is the point, from which develops the line, then the triangle and finally the square. As astrological aspects these translate as Point : Conjunction, Line : Opposition (180°), Triangle : Trine (120°) and Square : Square or Quadrature (90°). In meaning, the Point relates to Unity, Identity, Thesis, The Self. The Line or Opposition relates to Duality, Contrariety, Antithesis, the Not-Self. The Trine relates to Likeness, Affinity, Agreement. The Square relates to Dissimilarity, Disaffinity, Disagreement. These are the major aspects from which derive the Sextile (60°) an angle of minor affinity, the Semi-square (45°) and Sesqui-square (135°) angles of minor disaffinity. The conjunction relates to the Sun, the opposition to the Moon, the trine to Jupiter, the Square to Saturn, the sextile to Venus, the semi-square and sesqui-square to Mars.

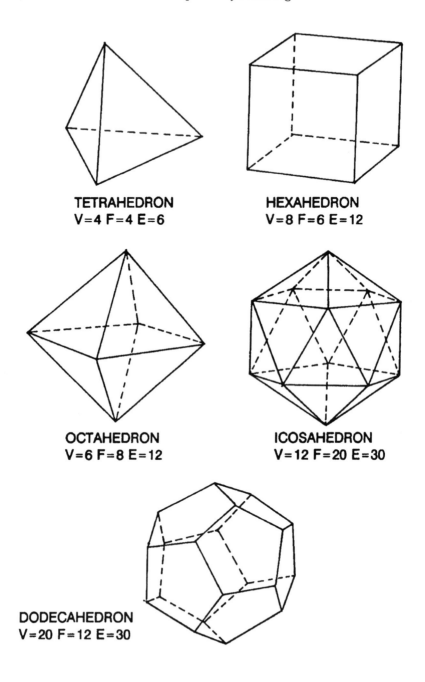

Speusippus, nephew of Plato, who later took over Plato's Academy, took the Pythagorean progression into the third dimension. The Point becomes the Line which then becomes first a Pyramid, then a Cube. The last two, the Pyramid and Cube relate as Tetrahedron and Hexahedron respectively to the first two of the five Perfect or Platonic Solids described in the Timaeus - the four-sided Tetrahedron, the six-sided Hexahedron, the eight-sided Octahedron, the twenty-sided Icosahedron and the twelve-sided Dodecahedron. These in turn relate to the four Elements - the Tetrahedron to Fire, the Hexahedron to Earth, the Octahedron to Air, the Icosahedron to Water, while the fifth, the Dodecahedron relates to the twelve signs of the zodiac and the cosmos itself. Of these 'perfect solids' the Tetrahedron, Hexahedron and the Dodecahedron were discovered by the Pythagoreans while the Octahedron and Icosahedron have been credited to Theaetetus the brilliant mathematician friend of Plato who was killed in 369 BC.

Figure 17 (opposite)

THE PLATONIC SOLIDS

All five solids may be inscribed within a sphere so that their vertices all touch the sphere. This is not possible with any other solid, hence the name 'Perfect Solids'. Here V = vertices, F = faces, E = edges. The Swiss Mathematician Leonhard Euler produced a formula, 'Euler's Formula', in which $V+F-E+2$ or vertices plus faces equals edges plus two. The solids were known to the Pythagoreans. In Plato they are associated with the 'elements' thus, Tetrahedron - Fire, Hexahedron - Earth, Octahedron - Air and Icosahedron - Water. The 12-sided Dodecahedron relates to the Zodiac and the Cosmos itself and is the Quinta Essentia or quintessence, the fifth substance or most perfect form pervading all things.

We have then the Trine aspect related to the Tetrahedron, the Square to the Hexahedron, the Sextile to the Octahedron, the semi- and sesqui-square to the Icosahedron and the Semi-Sextile (30°) since it is one twelfth of the circle to one facet of the Dodecahedron, the Pentagon. The Point and the Line from which both plane figures and solids take their origin represent the Conjunction and Opposition respectively. In our progression of meaning we have the conjunction representing Thesis, the opposition Antithesis. Grammatically the former stands for the Nominative Case, the latter for the Accusative Case. The Square, as the product of the coming together of Thesis and Antithesis, stands for the Genitive Case. It is an aspect of generation. Here we see Cancer (pregnancy, birth) linked by the square aspect (generation) to the proposition of the male sign Aries (Mars) and the acceptance of the female sign Libra (Venus). The trine aspect suggests a different version of generation. The square suggests the difficulty and pain of parturition. It is related to the element Earth and practicality and supposes the necessity of ensuring the continuation of the human race or the family line. Note that Cancer, or the fourth house, are symbolically adjacent to the Spindle of Necessity, the Meridian. The trine, on the other hand, is an aspect of facility and is related to the element Fire. It represents the ecstasy of intercourse, the urge of the 'libido' and its consummation. It relates the impulsive self (Aries - Ascendant) to the creative aspect of Leo and the Sun, or the fifth house of creativity which forms the central factor in the triangle - Aries - Leo - Sagittarius relating not to the Meridian but to the Horizon, not to necessity but to choice and free-will linking creativity (Leo) with personal impulse (Aries) and enthusiastic purpose (Sagittarius).[1] To return for a moment to the square. As an angle of generation it is seen in that astrological method whereby if the individual is represented by Aries his parents are symbolized by Cancer and Capricorn and his grandparents by Libra and Aries, all being at right angles thereby suggesting that a child is often more like a grandparent than a parent, since there is here a harmony in contrariety rather than a difference. The same goes for grandchildren. See diagram. This is, of course, a purely symbolic parentage. It suggests not how the actual parent or grandparent really is, but how the individual tends to see them.

Since this operation involving oppositions, squares and trines can be applied to any zodiacal sign as circumstances demands we can deduce meaning round the circle relating broadly to the zodiacal meanings already described. The lesser aspects help to fill out the picture. It is debateable whether the traditional meanings of the signs were originally arrived at by this method and the bare bones fleshed out by imagination, intuition and experience, but it is conceivable. The semi-sextile aspect which connects adjacent signs perform another function. In one sense, moving anti-clockwise from Aries through Taurus to Gemini round the circle there is a progressive complexity of meaning, while in the reverse direction we have a return to crudity and simplicity. Again in the anti-clockwise direction we have material causality, future built out of past, *post hoc propter hoc*, while clockwise we have not causality but logical consequence, the final cause as precedent for the formal cause (Aristotle). At another level the former relates to what is external or physical, the latter to what is internal or mental. Again the former direction suggests anticipation, the latter memory. Our twelvefold structure is capable of accommodating many levels of meaning. We can regard the zodiacal circle, for instance, as a potential progression for the individual from simple impulse (Aries) round the circle to an all-embracing understanding (Pisces). Though Pisces is at the end of the circle, in astrology there is no end and Aries starts off a new round. It is no accident that Aries has Pluto as an associated planet for Pluto rules Scorpio also, the sign of death and regeneration incorporating the idea of renewal and perhaps reincarnation. Aries is then the new beginning of another round. Plato was no stranger to the idea of re-incarnation as the Timaeus, the Myth of Er in the Republic and passages in the Phaedrus attest.

There is another series of aspects which together with its relationships, needs to be examined. This is the Quintile series discovered by Kepler. This series is arrived at by dividing the 360° circle not by three as in the trine, nor by four as in the square but by five. The Quintile of 72° spawns the semi-quintile (36°), the sesqui-quintile (108°) and the bi-quintile (144°). Like the other aspects these are also related to one of the Platonic Solids, in this case the Dodecahedron. Each face of the Dodecahedron is a Pentagon within which can be inscribed a five-pointed star, a Pentagram or Pentalpha - see diagram. The Pentagon as one twelfth of the Dodecagon and symbolic of a zodiacal sign as one twelfth of the cosmos is a figure to conjure with. If, as Galileo claimed, God geometrizes, then the Pentagon and its relations are splendid examples.

At the beginning of this book we set out to relate the solar system, its geometry and symbolism to categories of meaning. This was the view taken by Plato - that the cosmos was a logical, meaningful construction. Cosmos in Greek means 'arrangement'. We now learn from advances in quantum physics that the universe beloved of mechanistic science is not what we thought it was. It is neither material in itself, nor separate from us. It is a potential world only realized by our participation in it. It is part of us and we are part of it. Scientifically Heisenberg's 'Uncertainty Principle' is an example of this participation at sub-atomic level. Philosophically we have the authority of Kant in whose views participation was essential. Without it our world did not exist. Moreover, Kant claimed that space, time and causality were mental constructs arising out of man's participation in the world. In the Tarner Lectures at Cambridge fifty years ago the Nobel physicist Erwin Schroedinger said: '...the stuff from which our world picture is built is yielded exclusively from the sense organs as organs of the mind, so that every man's world picture is and always remains a construct of his mind and cannot be proved to have any other existence'. These convictions still form the basis of most philosophical thinking and are in harmony with present scientific discovery. Schroedinger went on to say that in the end multiplicity was only apparent and that in truth there was only one mind, which was, he emphasized, the doctrine of the Upanishads. Sir Arthur Eddington appeared to come to much the same conclusion, a conclusion in harmony with the philosophical basis of astrology.

A link illustrating our participation in the world is that of number and geometry. The rational mind is seen reflected in what we accept as material fact. This mathematical link is graphically evident when we consider the Dodecahedron and its relations. The Pentagon, as one face of the Dodecahedron, relates to the Pentagram which can be inscribed within it. Each leg of the isosceles triangles forming the Pentagram is cut in the exact ratio of the Golden Section by the other legs. The Golden Section otherwise known as the Divine Proportion is found mathematically by the formula $(1 + \sqrt{5})/2 = 1.618034$ and is usually abbreviated to Phi (ϕ). To Kepler this ratio was a 'precious jewel'. Note in the accompanying diagram that the angles of the isosceles triangles forming the Pentagram are quintiles and a semi-quintile so that the number five crops up not only in the sides of the Pentagon and in the $\sqrt{5}$ of the formula, but also in the five-pointed star of the Pentagram. The Golden Section was employed by Greek architects and sculptors as a ratio of rare beauty.

The sculptor Phidias made use of it and the ϕ of the formula is attributed to him. The proportions of the Parthenon also relate to the Golden Section and in the Renaissance many architects, notably Andrea Palladio, employed it.

Connected with the Golden Section is the Fibonacci Series in mathematics. Fibonacci (Filius Bonacci) otherwise known as Leonardo of Pisa discovered the series and published it in 1202 in his book Liber Abaci. Each term of the series after the first two is the sum of the preceding two terms, e.g., 1,1,2,3,5,8,13,21,34,55 and so on. The connection with the Golden Section is this; if we take one number and divide it by its preceding number we get ϕ or very near it. 55/34 = 1.6176, for example, but if we take higher numbers we get nearer and nearer still but never quite reach it exactly, for instance 144/89 = 1.6179 and 233/144 = 1.6180. This series crops up over and over again in nature relating mind to matter in an uncanny way.

Connected with both the Section and the Series is the logarithmic spiral or Spira Mirabilis. This relates to the Series in that the Fibonacci numbers plotted on squared paper produce a logarithmic spiral. Life develops according to a logarithmic rhythm. The period of menstruation is approximately twenty-eight days or one lunar month. Birth, on average, is 280 days or ten lunar months after conception. Childhood ends with 2,800 days or 100 lunar months, i.e., 7.7 years, followed by adolescence, maturity and old age lasting 28,000 days, 1000 lunar months or 77.7 years. The figures, of course, are approximate and on average. it, nevertheless, is an index of the speed of entelechy in physical development - very rapid in the embryo, less so in childhood and very much slowed down in old age and is an explanation of why when one is a child time seems to drag interminably and yet races by when we are old.

The logarithmic spiral has a, possibly coincidental, relationship through Fechner's Law with the way we interpret our world through the five senses (the number five again). The German psychologist Fechner found that the response to a stimulus was proportional to the log of that stimulus - our sensitivity to light and sound, for instance - depends on the log of the stimulus so that we can draw an exponential logarithmic spiral to illustrate the proportional sensitivity of eye and ear to the increase or decrease of the stimulus. Fechner's law is not exact for stimulus/response in all circumstances but it is a useful working rule. In nature exactitudes are not individual but statistical - they may be wrong for an individual case but surprisingly accurate for a thousand. The logarithmic spiral crops up again in the geological time scale, our concept of time past being proportional to the logarithm of the actual time elapsed as will be seen if we scale out the lengths of geological periods - quaternary, tertiary, mesozoic, palaeozoic and pre-Cambrian.

In zoology also the spiral plays a notable part, the horns, beaks, claws and tusks of animals being conspicuous examples. The shell of the Nautilus is an almost perfect logarithmic curve and as it develops its growth continues to follow the logarithmic spiral. In botany flowers such as the daisy, sunflower and aster have centres made up of florets arranged in intersecting logarithmic spirals. In the daisy family the numbers of ray-florets also correspond to the Fibonacci Series. In the sun-flower head the series and the spiral are combined.

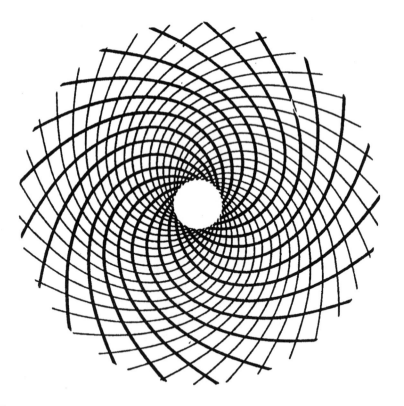

Figure 18 SPIRA MIRABILIS - The Logarithmic Spiral
The spiral pattern seen in the sunflower head. Two sets of spirals are interwoven. If these are counted it will be found that they are twenty-one clockwise and thirty-four anti-clockwise spirals, 21 and 34 both being Fibonacci numbers.

The Fibonacci Series and the Spira Mirabilis are again combined in the semitones of the chromatic scale in music. The Series is related to the sequence of white and black notes on the piano keyboard and to the distance between the frets on a guitar. Even within the instrument with which we hear music, the ear, the cochlea roughly corresponds with a logarithmic spiral. In botany, again, Fibonacci crops up in phyllotaxis, the arrangement of leaves on the stems of plants. A curious discovery is that it also relates to the heredity of the drone bee. The drone has a mother but no father and so has five great-great-grandparents. The parents of these great-great-grandparents are eight in number so that now we have 5 + 8 = 13, thirteen being the number of all the ancestor's grandparents while five, eight and thirteen are all Fibonacci numbers. This ubiquitous series occurs again in the breeding of rabbits. Just how it does so is too complicated to set out here but those interested will find an explanation in 'The Divine Proportion' by H.E. Huntley which explains in detail what has here only been touched upon. Finally we can go to the limits of magnitude and still find traces of this strange pair, the Series and the Spiral. The Galaxies and Spiral Nebulae correspond in shape to the Logarithmic Spiral while, at the other extreme the Fibonacci Series appears in the histories of an atomic electron.

The point of this apparent digression into simple geometry and mathematics is to demonstrate that not only can the *a priori* mind be related to structures based on the earth's rotation on itself and on its rotation round the circle but that tangible phenomena can be seen to relate, mathematically at least, to the structures forming the foundations of astrology and, indeed of astronomy. Nature is shot through with mathematics as writers such as D'Arcy Wentworth Thompson ('On Growth and Form') have abundantly shown.† The Section, the Series and the Spiral all relate to the fifth Platonic Solid, the Dodecahedron, symbol of the cosmos itself and the key figure in Plato's cosmology. Mathematics itself has, of course, long divided

---

† This morphic relationship between mathematics and natural phenomena has apparently taken a new turn with the advent of 'chaos theory' in which, underlying the randomness which appeared to lie at the base of all existence, mathematicians have discovered an exploding series of self-generating patterns of great beauty and bewildering intricacy. Behind disorder there lurks a highly coherent order of a kind hitherto undreamt of. Chaos swallows order and, in turn, gives birth to it - the identity and coincidence of opposites once again.

mathematicians as to whether mathematics was purely a construction of the human mind, or whether it was external and independent of it. Undoubtedly it appears in the phenomenal world and we are constantly coming upon it there, but is it there as part of the world and we recognise it, or do we put it there? We are once again impaled on the horns of a dualistic dilemma. The answer is, surely, both - or rather we are dealing with two aspects of the same. They are the same because we and our world are the same, part of each other, dependent on each other, creators of each other - one.

We must not get carried away. What may appear nicely sewn up is not necessarily true. What we have before us is a paradigm, not the Holy Grail. But it is, we submit, a paradigm worth examining, a practical working hypothesis for experiment, remembering that what we are dealing with is potential rather than actual. We have to bear in mind, too, that categories and structures of meaning are Janus-faced and can be either strait-jackets for thought or springboards for discovery. Astrology can be a closed, charmed, incestuous circle as in the popular version or alternatively an open-ended stimulus to the mind, throwing up new and unexpected relationships.

We have made use of the astrological aspects to show how the meaning of zodiacal signs may be deduced, and how they relate to such geometrical figures as the triangle, square and Platonic Solids. In practice, however, their main use is to provide a meaningful relationship between what is symbolized by one planet and another or between a planet and the Meridian or Horizon. The aspect not only brings the two together but the type of aspect qualifies the nature of the link. Jupiter in square aspect to Saturn emphasizes the differences between the two and since Jupiter and Saturn are already antipathetic by nature this aspect piles Pelion upon Ossa. Jupiter trine Saturn, however, presents a different picture. Here the control and stability of Saturn supports the enthusiasm and enterprise of Jupiter, or conversely the enthusiasm of Jupiter enlivens and energises the principles of Saturn. Generally the inner and more personal factors - the Ascendant, Midheaven, Sun, Moon, Mercury, Venus and Mars are considered to be potentially affected by the outer and more impersonal factors - Jupiter, Saturn, Uranus, Neptune and Pluto - but the link, as ever with astrology, is two-way. In natal astrology preference should be given to the personal factors. In mundane astrology, or the astrology of groups or nations, the more impersonal factors come to the fore.

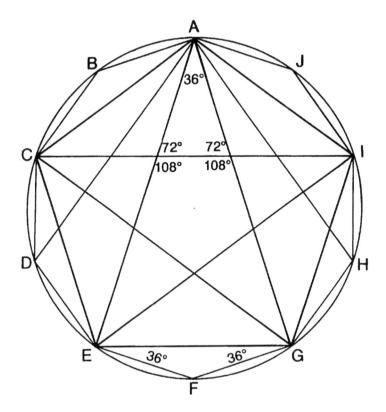

Figure 19

<u>THE CIRCLE DIVIDED BY KEPLER</u>
The Quintile Series of Aspects

A - B = 36°	Angle AEC = 36°	Angles of pentagons = 108°
A - C = 72°	AEG = 72°	
A - D = 108°	CEG = 144°	Angles of triangles = 36°, 72°, 72°
A - E = 144°		

The central pentagon within the larger pentagon ACEGI is equivalent to one face of the Dodecahedron, forming the centre of the pentagram. If the angles of the central pentagon are joined we get a further pentagram inscribed within it, and so on ad infinitum. The diagonals of the pentagram star are cut in the ratio of the Golden Section. The pentagram and Golden Section are related to the Logarithmic Spiral and the Fibonacci Series in mathematics, and thence to the geometry of nature. (See p. 113)

An aspect does not have to be accurate to the degree, though it is more 'potent' if it is. There is a latitude of effectiveness known as an 'orb' within which the aspect is deemed to be operative. There is, however, no general consensus concerning orbs and opinions vary. Perhaps an average of 8° for conjunction, opposition, trine and square, 4° for sextile, semi- and sesqui-square, 2° for sextiles and 1° or 1½° for the quintile series might be a rough guide. These are operative for the natal chart but not for the developed chart in time, involving 'progressions' (see note), where the orbs should be cut to about one degree. The aspect is reckoned either before exactitude (applying) or after (separating), the faster factor applying to or separating from the slower.

We have dealt briefly with the meanings of the major and minor aspects but not, so far, with the quintile series. This series relates, as we have seen, to the number five, the Pentagon, the Pentagram and the Dodecahedron. Five is a central number in the series 123/456/789. It is also the central number in the creative or generative triangle 1 - 5 - 9 relating to the fifth house of creation. It relates to the Golden Section as a number of balance and equilibrium. It corresponds to our first computer system, our five fingers for counting. Through the Logarithmic Spiral it can be connected with the five senses and with Fechner's Law of stimulus/response. In addition five represents the 'Quinta Essentia', the quintessence of anything. The Pythagoreans regarded the five-pointed star, the Pentagram, as an emblem of health. In alchemical terms the Pentagram was the symbol of magical power. Balance, creativity, health, power and their opposites, imbalance, destructiveness, ill health and misuse of power are all conjured up in this number and its relations. It tends to occur repeatedly as quintile aspects in the horoscopes of such people as Mozart, Hitler, and of seriously disturbed people such as schizophrenics. Anyone with a battery of quintiles in his chart is potentially, and again we caution potentially, someone out of the ordinary, for better or worse.

There is another system of linkage which need not involve aspects. This is the mid-point system developed in the last fifty years in Germany and in this country but which owes its origin to Guido Bonatti in the thirteenth century, court astrologer to the Emperor Frederick II. A mid-point is a degree unoccupied by any factor but lying mid-way between two planets. Any third planet aspecting this degree will combine the meanings of the three planets involved.

These combined meanings have been tabulated in 'The Combination of Stellar Influences' (COSI for short) by the late Reinhold Ebertin. Although this method is not germane to the general argument we have attempted to set out, it is mentioned here so that readers may understand such combinations when they occur in charts to be examined later.

VIII. SUN, MOON AND PLANETS

'This is the great function of symbols: to point beyond themselves....
to open up levels of the human mind of which we otherwise are not
aware'.

Paul Tillich

'The examination of symbolic structures is a work not of *reduction*
but of *integration*. One compares and contrasts two expressions of
a symbol not in order to reduce them to a single, pre-existent
expression, but in order to discover the process by which a structure
is capable of enriching its meanings'.

Mircea Eliade

The sun, moon and planets stand as symbols or vehicles for concepts, in Pauli's words 'image-formers'.[1] They may be taken as general principles or universals characterizing life in all its aspects. Psychologically they may be considered as 'propensities'. Again, we must remember, we are in the realm of potentialities, not facts. What follows is a bare list of principles, but one must read between the lines. The symbols are capable of accommodating a vast range of concepts and, as symbols, there is no necessity to list them all even if one could. As Tillich says, symbols 'point beyond themselves'. We show in what follows which way they are pointing. What particular meaning may be apposite to any occasion is left to the enquirer. Moreover it should be remembered that the more general and vague the meaning the more chance there is of its being apposite, the more particular and precise the meaning the greater the chance of its being inaccurate. In our attempt to narrow down the range of meaning from the vagueness of the universal, through the categories to the particular we should have some idea of how far we should go and where to stop. We are helped in this exercise when faced with an actual event for the nature of the event itself will single out the relevant category or particular for us, but where there is no such event and we are considering a chart *in vacuo* without knowledge of the attendant circumstances the above caveat applies.

In considering planetary meaning the *coniunctio oppositorum*, the coming together of opposites and the ideas of complementarity, equality and union are important. The Sun relates to the day, the Moon to the night, the Sun to what is open, the Moon to what is hidden, the Sun to the conscious, the Moon to the sub-conscious, the Sun to the male, the Moon to the female, the Sun to the assertive, the Moon to the receptive, the Sun to the Yang, the Moon to the Yin. Although the Sun is the largest feature of the solar system, the Moon the smallest, in astrology they are regarded as equals balancing each other and, indeed, in the sky they appear to us of equal size as is evidenced by an eclipse of the Sun when the Moon's disc exactly obliterates that of the Sun. Everyone, of whichever sex, bears within him or herself both the solar and the lunar principle much as, in Jungian psychology the male's subconscious nourishes the *anima*, the female's the *animus*. In astrology sexual difference is balanced by sexual equality. The fact that in our society male values are considered more important than female ones is out of kilter with astrology. This balance and complementarity is again emphasized in the pairs Venus - Mars, Jupiter - Saturn, Uranus - Neptune. These pairs are all rulers of adjacent signs and are what may be called 'intrinsic' opposites. There are also 'extrinsic' opposites in which the planets are rulers of opposite signs.[2] Mercury which is not one of an adjacent pair has extrinsic opposites in Jupiter and Neptune, while moon opposes Saturn and Sun opposes Uranus. Mars and Venus partake of both kinds of opposition intrinsic and extrinsic.

The difference between the two kinds of opposites is that the intrinsic type are symbolically 'electro-magnetic' and compulsive since they embrace signs of different polarity - plus and minus. The extrinsic kind, on the other hand, could be described as 'gravitational' since, being of the same polarity, there is a certain likeness despite the opposition. The difference is not so abrupt and the possibility of harmony in contrariety is ever present.

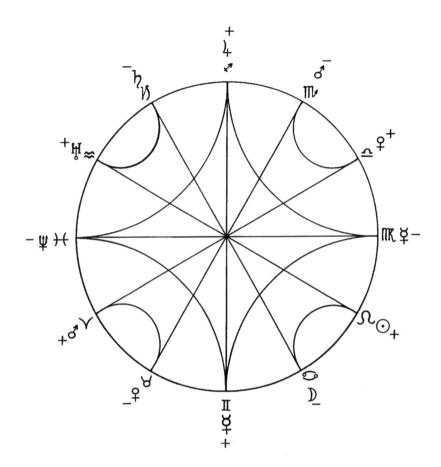

Figure 20 - EXTRINSIC AND INTRINSIC OPPOSITES

Extrinsic opposites are connected by diameters. Intrinsic opposites are connected by arcs. It will be seen that Venus and Mars, Mercury and Jupiter and Mercury and Neptune are connected by both diameters and arcs and are therefore both extrinsic and intrinsic opposites. Extrinsic diameters connect Plus to Plus, Minus to Minus. Intrinsic arcs connect Plus to Minus.

In the following delineations 'Centrifugal' is used as the physical counterpart of the psychological 'Extrovert', 'Centripetal' as the physical counterpart of 'Introvert'.

THE MOON: Negative. Centripetal. Introvert. Cyclothyme. Viscerotonic.

The Moon is a feminine symbol of great antiquity, relating to both mother, wife and femininity in general, while its monthly period relates to menstruation. Beyond this, as categories of meaning depending from a wide-ranging and fertile universal, we can list the following: Receptivity. Enclosing. Containing. Clasping. Holding. Cradling. Rocking, swaying movement. Rhythmic change. Care and protection. Sensation. Reflection. Moods, Emotions. Imagination. Memory. The subconscious. Instinct. Habit. Sentiment. Nostalgia. Family. Home. Family tradition and custom. Clannishness. Maternal instinct. Pregnancy. Birth. Childhood.

In a man's horoscope the Moon may stand for his mother or for his wife, or 'anima'. It also represents his more sensitive, receptive side and the way in which he tends to react to, or be impressed by, others rather than to impress them (Sun). Both Sun and Moon have a rather more general significance than the planets. Since they are the basic positive and negative factors and negative factors, when in relation with another planet they help to bring it into polar prominence. The Sun tends to strengthen and externalize that planet's symbolized qualities; the Moon internalizes or implies a reaction to its qualities. For example, Sun-Venus may mean outward expression of feelings, love, affection and so on, whereas Moon-Venus may indicate inward feelings of affection or love.

Breasts. Womb. Stomach. The Rib-cage. Pancreas. Digestive and uterine trouble. The ovaries and female hormone function. The placenta. Ovulation. Menstruation. Conception. Parturition. Cell cytoplasm. The lymphatic system. Collagen diseases. The Sun and Moon relate to the primitive parts of the brain - the Diencephalon, in its positive and negative aspects. The cerebral cortex relates to Mercury. The eyes as negative, instinctive receptors - 'seeing' or 'registering'.

THE SUN: Positive. Centrifugal. Extrovert. Cyclothyme. Somatotonic.

Vitality. Libido. Élan vital. Warmth of manner. Geniality. Power. Generative power. Creative power. Centralized power. Natural authority. Command. Domination. Organization. Self-expression. Self-assertion. Arrogance. Pride. Self-confidence. Risk. Spirit. Mettle. Drive for recognition and acclaim.
In family life the Sun stands for the father, paternal feeling, the urge for procreation, fatherhood. In a woman's horoscope it may stand for her father, or for her husband, or for her 'animus'. It may also represent the masculine side of a woman as well as the desire to express herself and make her presence felt. Where the Moon encloses and protects, centring on the family (centripetal) the Sun reaches out, impressing itself on its milieu, seeking wider horizons whether mental or physical (Centrifugal).

The Heart. The Pericardium. Heart muscle. The circulatory system. The Aorta and Vena Cava. The heat maintenance of the body. The thoracic vertebrae. The back. The spinal column. The testes and male hormone function. The cell nucleus. The eyes as positive instruments of perception involving conscious purpose and direction (looking, peering, examining, focusing as opposed to seeing or registering - Moon). Cardiac disfunction. Bradycardia. Tachycardia. Cardiac arrest. Coronary heart disease. Angina pectoris. Fatty degeneration. Hypertrophy. Palpitation. Valvular disease. Stroke. Aneurysm.

It will no doubt be remarked that there is an anatomical location present in most of the above, there is a functional or physiological connection in others (Stroke), while analogy and affinity account for the rest, (the cell nucleus, the testes and the eyes). In all the succeeding planetary attributions the static or anatomical, the dynamic, functional or physiological, and the claims of analogy and affinity should be taken into account.

MERCURY: Neutral. Schizothyme. Cerebrotonic.

The reasoning function of the mind. Intelligence. Logic. Rational thought, speech, language, writing, teaching. Means of communication, movement, change, exchange. Literacy, numeracy, cleverness, versatility. Ingenuity, curiosity, sophistication. Analysis, critical ability. Skill, precision, technical ability, expertise, craftsmanship, specialization. Gesticulation, nervous behaviour, nervous oscillation, worry. The mercurial type tends to be over-meticulous and sometimes obsessed with detail, over-precise and something of a perfectionist; or can be hypercritical and a bit of a hair-splitter.

The reasoning functions of the mind centred in the cerebral cortex. The motor and sensory areas in the cortex. The hands and fingers as instruments of communication, indication, or for manipulation as precision tools. The nerves generally. Motor-nerve may be represented by Mercury-Mars, sensory nerve by Mercury-Venus. The tongue as organ of speech and articulation. Joint articulations. The limbs generally. The trachea, bronchi and vocal chords. The lungs as instruments of oxygen-carbon dioxide exchange, speech and respiration. Intermittent, variable, flexible or oscillatory movement, as contrasted with the undulating, swaying movement of the Moon. Nervous tremor, tics, stammer or other speech impediment. The thyroid gland. The assimilative function of the small intestine. Peristalsis. Digestive troubles due to nerves. The duodenum and duodenal ulcer. Respiratory trouble. Asthma. Hay fever. Pneumonia. Mercury is also an indicator of general health from a functional point of view.

VENUS: Negative. Centripetal. Introvert. Cyclothyme. Viscerotonic.

Attraction. Attachment. Union. Association. Complementarity. Adhesion. Reciprocity. Sharing. Levelling. Equalising. Doubling. Pairing. Intimacy. Co-habitation. Marriage. Partnership. Mutuality. Conductivity. Ductility. Receptivity. Nubility. Mutual attraction. Love and sex. Where the Moon stands for conception and birth, Venus stands for intercourse, whether sexual or social. Deliberation. Weighing the balance. Choice. Evaluation. Appreciation. Co-operation. Aesthetic sensitivity. Beauty. Form. Proportion. Anything taken in - supplies, food, property, money, earnings, acquisitions. Accumulation. Comfort. Ease. Luxury. Sweetness, roundness, softness, gentleness.

In a man's horoscope Venus may stand for the feminine side of his nature, for his desire for completion, his search for a complement, his need for a balance-weight, his wife or mistress. Venus, like the Moon, is a traditional feminine symbol but whereas the Moon corresponds with the protective, maternal, procreative aspects of female activity, Venus relates to the connubial, attractive, sexual, seductive and co-operative side.

Soft tissues generally. The balancing mechanism of the body. The skin, not only in its cosmetic function, but as organ of sensation, and as regulator of temperature between body and environment. The maintenance of the acid-base balance, plasma balance and blood sugar balance. The kidneys. The filtering and exchange of fluids. Osmosis. The cerebellum. The balance of muscular function - synergy. The balancing mechanism in the semicircular canals in the inner ear. The parathyroids. The neck. The waist. The lumbar area. Female sexual function. Hormonal function. The ovum. Venous blood flow in the veins. Cell protoplasm. Venereal diseases. Skin diseases. Orifices and vessels for taking things in and passing things through: tubes, ducts, sleeves, sheaths, apertures - in contradistinction to lunar vessels which hold and contain. Digestive tract, mouth, throat, vagina, umbilicus, auditory meatus. Mitigating, assuaging, pacifying action. Lenitive, soothing, palliatives and demulcents.

MARS: Positive. Centrifugal. Extrovert. Schizothyme. Somatotonic.

Forceful nature. Drive. Activity. Aggression. Strife. Daring. Pugnacity. Impudence. Vigour. Roughness. Harshness. Sharpness and penetration as opposed to the roundness and receptivity of Venus.

Mars stands symbolically for the attack and penetration of the sword, the knife, the surgeon's scalpel, for the phallus and sexual energy (as opposed to the sensuality, feeling and receptivity of Venus). Where Venus heals, Mars wounds. Where Mars penetrates Venus engulfs. If Mars is the sword, Venus is the sheath. If Mars means war, Venus brings peace.

Unlike the equalizing propensities of Venus, Mars tries to get the upper hand, to force issues, to demand things from life, to self assertion, to initiating projects, to fighting for self advancement in every department of life from social relationships to war. The deliberation and consideration of Venus is replaced by impetuosity, union is replaced by division. Reciprocity becomes not sharing but hitting back. It will be recognized that Mars in the seventh house is no recipe for a trouble-free partnership.

Anger. Passion. Desire. Irritability. Excitement. Choler. Impatience. Forceful activity. Foolhardiness. Destructiveness. Bravery. Ruthlessness. Mars, like the Sun, stands as a male symbol, but more specifically in a sexual aspect. In a woman's horoscope Mars may stand for her masculine side, also for the qualities she seeks from her mate to complement her and, by extension, it may stand for her husband or lover.

Harshness. Roughness. Sharpness. Belligerence. Aggression.

Muscle generally, but especially 'striated'[3] or voluntary muscle (heart muscle is represented by the Sun and involuntary muscle by Jupiter). The male sexual function. The penis. Spermatozoon. Adrenal glands. Arterial blood flow. Red corpuscles of the blood as oxygen carriers to the tissues. Oxygen (the word comes form the Greek 'oxys' meaning 'sharp'). The head and nose, sacrum and coccyx. Acute diseases. Fevers. Inflammation. Irritation. Accident. Injury. Operation. Haemorrhage. Cuts. Wounds. Burns. Scalds. Bites. Stings. Acute pain - sharp, cutting, searing, sore or burning. Ulcers. Acute infections. Inoculation. Surgery. Abrasive, barbed or punctate wounds. Elimination. Excretion. Ejaculation. Excision.

Sun, Moon and Planets

JUPITER: Positive. Centrifugal. Extrovert. Cyclothyme. Somatotonic.

The typical 'jovial' temperament. Optimistic. Expansive. Ebullient. Enthusiastic. Exaggerative. Proud. Generous. Overestimation. Squandermania. Megalomania. Euphoria. Elation. Self-indulgence. Wastefulness. Over confident. Pomposity. Humbug. Ostentation. Swagger. Pretension. Impulsiveness. Intuitive foresight. Speculation. The urge to seize every opportunity, to take a chance, to gamble. The effect of Jupiter is to increase or exaggerate the qualities of any planet associated with it.

Smooth or involuntary muscle. The posterior pituitary gland controlling the involuntary muscles. The lower limbs especially hips and thighs. The liver in its glycogen forming and storing function. Liver trouble. Gout. Diseases of surfeit and over indulgence. Fat. Adipose tissue generally. Disturbances of carbohydrate metabolism - hyperglycaemia and glycosuria. Excess function of any organ. Hypertrophy. Distension. Inflation. Dilatation. Tumescence. Elasticity. Resilience. High blood pressure. The posterior pituitary gland secretes vaso-pressin which both stimulates smooth muscle and raises blood pressure. Muscle may be represented thus: Mars - striped or voluntary muscle. Mars-Jupiter - Smooth or involuntary muscle. Mars-Sun - Spiral or vortical heart muscle.

SATURN: Negative. Centripetal. Introvert. Schizothyme. Cerebrotonic.

The typical 'saturnine' temperament. Pessimistic. Frugal. Ascetic. Restrictive. Serious. Earnest. Self-controlled. Cautious. Sceptical. Restrained. Correct. Authoritarian. A stickler for law and order. Conventional. Ambitious. Gravity. Sobriety. Stoicism. 'Backbone'. Inhibition. Shyness. Doubt. Fear. Austerity. Abstinence. Parsimoniousness. Selfishness. Indifference. Coolness. Coldness. Inflexibility. Hardness. Stubbornness. Steadiness. Application. Persistence. Endurance. Rigidity. Orthodoxy. Duty. Responsibility. Control. Prohibition. Censorship. Discipline. Codes of behaviour. Alienation. Isolation. Depression. Frustration.

Obstacles. Barriers. Limits. Material aims and ends. Structure. Form. Regularity. Order. Law. Conformity. Uniformity. Routine. Tradition. Inheritance. Standards. Norms. Touchstones. Bases. Formalities. Foundations. Supports. Props. Steadying. Underpinning.

From a psychological point of view Saturn is perhaps the most important planetary symbol. In one sense it relates to Freud's concept of the 'super-ego'; in another to Jung's idea of the 'shadow'. In general it represents that which most impedes one's actions or emotions. It also indicates the conventions, traditions, rules and regulations by which we live.[†]

Saturn may stand in the horoscope for one's father as the Moon may stand for one's mother, but if so it is for the father as a rather austere, disciplinary or distant figure; the father as out-going encouraging paterfamilias is represented by the Sun. It may also stand for anyone in control or in a position of authority - superior officer, boss, or indeed either parent if parental control is seen as exercised by both. Outside the home it may stand for the legal authority, the law or the government.

We have considered parenthood as relating to the Moon (mother) and Sun and Saturn (father) but, more fundamentally, Sun, Moon and Saturn may relate to either parent - the Sun to the encouraging, outgoing aspects of parenthood (of either sex), the Moon to the closer, more protective, receptive aspects, and Saturn to the more remote, disciplinary or restrictive characteristics of parenthood. In one-parent families or where one parent has died the characteristics of Saturn come to the fore indicating limitation, increased weight of responsibility and the need for discipline falling on the remaining parent. Where Jupiter signifies expansion, growth and development, Saturn suggests limitation, contraction and a slowing down of natural

---

[†] Saturn relates to the concept of 'conscience' and its development:

Conscience	- external voice of authority - fear, frustration.	Must
	- internal, propriate voice of authority (Allport)	↓
↓	- internalized voice of ones contemporaries.	
	- private codes of virtue, sin, obligation.	
	- an inclusive path of life requiring discipline,	↓
	self-guidance and direction.	Ought

Similar meanings are applicable to the sign Capricorn.

processes. Rigidity. Resistance. Heaviness. Solidity. Slowness. Narrowness. Concentration. Dryness. Dullness. Frigidity. Insulation. Loneliness. Cutting oneself off from others.

Bone. Cartilage. The anterior pituitary gland controlling the skeletal system and bone formation. Calcification. Sedimentation. Sclerosis. Acromegaly. Osteoporosis. Rickets. Osteoarthritis. Ankylosed joints. The spleen. Haemopoiesis. Limiting, chronic or crippling diseases. Deficiency diseases. Ageing. Wear and tear. Hardening. Crepitus. Arteriosclerosis. The control mechanism in the central nervous system in the spinal cord. Lead poisoning. Constipation. Blockage. Accidents through falls or by pressure - crushing, bruising. Atrophy. Diminished function. Deafness. Aches. Loss of movement. Skeletal anomalies and deformities. Orthopaedics. Persistent dull, grinding nagging pain (as opposed to the acuteness of Mars). The knees. The skin as protective integument, the 'stratum corneum', the nails and teeth. Saturn is usually involved with Neptune in cases of paralysis. 'Limping' or 'hobbling' is Saturnian and a crutch or a prosthesis a Saturnian appliance.

URANUS: Positive. Centrifugal. Extrovert. Schizothyme. Cerebrotonic.

With Uranus we enter the realm of the sub- or super-normal. Uranus illustrates centrifugal force 'flying off at a tangent'. Eccentric movement.† A break with the normal, conventional way of life, if

---

† In the realm of art, cubism, futurism, dadaism and abstract art generally are typical Uranian departures. 'Musique concrète' and electronic music have also Uranian elements. In literature the 'pun', 'spoonerisms' and neologisms are obviously Uranian. Joyce's 'Ulysses' and 'Finnegans Wake' as also the writings of Jorge Luis Borges, nonsense rhymes and the Japanese 'Haiku' are Uranian in type. Utopias - Thomas More, Campanella (The City of the Sun), H.G. Wells (The Time Machine) are also Uranian in concept. Alice in Wonderland has more than a dash of both Uranus and Neptune.
  In quantum physics Uranian symbolism is evident in Heisenberg's 'Uncertainty Principle'. In the rapidly developing 'chaos theory' of the last few years the dazzlingly beautiful development of 'fractals' out of chaos discovered by the mathematician Mandelbrot is again typically Uranian. (J Gleick: *Chaos*, Abacus '93).

not a radical 'breakthrough' into revolutionary new ideas. Saturn represents the limit of normality and conventionality while the three extra-Saturnian planets Uranus, Neptune and Pluto introduce an element of abnormality for better or worse. They are often prominent in the charts of men of genius on the one hand and of cranks or the mentally disturbed on the other. Everybody has the capacity for such deviation from normality but for most it merely remains as unrealized potential, or perhaps a tendency to behave unusually in a certain direction while being perfectly conventional in all other respects. Uranus may also stand for 'saltatory becoming' a phrase used by the psychologist Gordon Allport to illustrate a sudden unexpected switch of personality or behaviour due to latent capacities suddenly surfacing and taking over.

High nervous tension. Galvanic, spasmodic action. Unorthodox behaviour and belief. Sudden switches of direction and polarity. Unpredictability. Revolt against authority. Radical change or upheaval. Revolution. Break with the past, tradition or convention. Originality. Invention. Lightning intuition. Archimedes cry of 'Eureka'. Sudden conversion (e.g., the road to Damascus). Sudden, intuitive, irrational thought. Intuitive appreciation of apparently logically unrelated principles. The Zen 'Koan'. Scientific discovery. Progressive, revolutionary or merely cranky ideas. Anarchy. Iconoclasm. Heterodoxy. Paradox. As well as the radically new Uranus may equally relate to the very old - palaeontology or archaeology for instance, going back to remote origins. The German prefix 'Ur...' as in 'Urahn' (great grandfather) contains the ideas of great age, originality and primitivity. Goethe's 'Urpflanze' (original plant form) is typically Uranian in concept. If Saturn stands for the old, Uranus stands for the new, or the very old. In mythology Uranus was Saturn's father.

Great independence. Odd, erratic, eccentric or brusque behaviour. Great nervous excitement. Nervous shock or breakdown. Nervous compulsions. Paranoia. Electro-convulsive (shock) treatment. Bizarre, irrelevant ideas. Irrational hostility. Compulsive attraction. Spasmodic, highly strung, compulsive and unstable relationships. Rupture of relationships. Divorce. Where Venus in relationship with Saturn may indicate steady, permanent, conventional unions, or coolness of affection or sexual frigidity according to context, Venus with Uranus may stand for unexpected attachments, an eccentric choice (e.g., homosexuality, inter-racial or inter-religious unions, or extreme difference in the ages of the partners), great sensual excitability, a compulsively romantic love affair, or breaks, rupture of relationship and divorce.

In the realm of physics the critical instability of Uranus is evident in radioactive substances, especially uranium,† and in atomic fission. In biology it symbolizes mutation. The quantum theory and the theory of relativity with which Max Planck and Einstein radically changed our view of the universe are instances of Uranian principle. In the field of sub-atomic physics causality (Saturn) can no longer be universally demonstrated and a certain irrationality and unpredictability (Heisenberg's 'uncertainty principle') makes its appearance in typically Uranian fashion. The metal uranium with its critical instability, explosive quality and radioactive potential is typical of the symbolism also.

Nervous excitability. The nerve synapses within the spinal cord. Increased, galvanic reflex action. Nervous tics, cramps, spasms. Spastic conditions. Spastic paralysis. The Grey matter of the spinal cord. The sino-auricular node in the heart (the 'pacemaker') as the site of origin of cardiac contraction regulating heart beat. Heart-block. Auricular flutter. Fibrillation. The anterior pituitary in its gonado-tropic function responsible for the development of both sexes.
Paranoia. Shock. Nervous breakdown. Epilepsy. Seizures. Sudden, unexpected disorders. Unusual or undiagnosed ailments. Unusual forms of therapy. Alternative therapy. Immediate surgical intervention. Together with Mars it is an indicator of operation.

It will be seen that Uranus has a certain affinity with Mercury, and indeed Uranus is considered as a higher octave of Mercury. But here, with Uranus, the nerve of Mercury is tensed to snapping point; the reason of Mercury is surpassed by lightning intuition. Mercury is logical, Uranus is heuristic. It goes beyond logic into paradox, invention and discovery; or it goes beyond reason into unreason and mental aberration.

---

† Uranium was discovered by Klaproth in 1789 who named it after Uranus. In 1896 Becquerel discovered it was radioactive.

NEPTUNE: Negative. Centripetal. Introvert. Cyclothyme. Viscerotonic.

Hypersensitivity. Unusual capacity for receptivity, sympathy and empathy. Suggestibility. Great imagination. Fantasy. Illusion. Delusion. Deception. Hypersusceptibility to outside influences, 'atmospheres', 'vibrations', weather changes, narcotic, gas, smells, intoxicants, poisons, hypnotism. Extreme flexibility, lability, exhaustion, dissipation, disintegration, dissolution, softening. Physically Neptune is the weakest planet. Mentally, however, it ranges further, wider and deeper than any other. Einstein had his Sun and Midheaven in the Neptunian sign Pisces with the Sun closely aspecting Neptune.
Abstraction. Immateriality. Idealism. Otherworldliness. Enlightenment. Absentmindedness. Dreaminess. Vagueness. Mystical states. The 'Oceanic feeling'. Preoccupation with ideas and theories, with what is limitless, unknowable and eternal.
Renunciation. Resignation. Retreat. Escape. Self-sacrifice. Surrender. Indiscriminate. Philanthropy. Charitableness. A general indiscriminate fellow feeling for the 'underdog', the unfortunate, regardless of class, creed, colour, race or social position. A potentiality for insight, second sight, clairvoyance, visions, telepathy, 'voices', dowsing, mediumship and all that comes under what is known as psi-phenomena or extra-sensory perception. Unorthodox religious belief of an all-encompassing nature, the opposite of narrow orthodoxy or 'fundamentalism'. Prophetic. Superstitious. The aim is understanding in its deepest sense but owing to its proclivity for neither recognising nor complying with limits its belief may degenerate into superstition and deception.
Permissiveness (with Neptune 'anything goes', the subject finding its extremely difficult to say 'no' to anything). Chaotic conditions - no limits, no structure, no order.† In contrast to Uranus there is no

---

† In art surrealism is typically Neptunian - Salvador Dali, de Chirico, Picabia, Magritte. El Greco also had a powerful Neptunian slant. In music - Chopin, Ravi Shankar, Tchaikovsky. In poetry - Rimbaud, Francis Thompson, Rilke. G.K. Chesterton's 'The Man who was Thursday', automatic writing, spirit writing, pentecostal glossolalia, the Book of Revelations, The Pseudo Dionysius, writings of the mystics - St. John of the Cross, Traherne, William Law, Ruysbroeck, the Sufi poetry, the Tao te Ching, Orphism. (continued overleaf)

revolt against order or structure, only an inability to bring it about for oneself, or a tendency to drop-out from any order set up by others, by 'the establishment' or by convention. Many 'drop-outs' or tramps display obvious Neptunian qualities. If a Neptunian likes drink he may have a tendency to become a 'soak' or alcoholic. Others have a tendency to drug-addiction or a strong revulsion against drugs, alcohol or narcotics of any sort.

People with Neptune prominent are often very suggestible and should prove easy subjects for hypnotism, or if they are aware of this, difficult subjects since they may have a fear of losing control of themselves. They tend to have a feeling for anything which has rhythm and fluidity such as music, dance and poetry, also the sea. Where Uranus has an affinity with Mercury, Neptune has a similarity with Venus as its 'higher octave' (see accompanying diagram). With Neptune, however, the love and fellow feeling of Venus is extended to embrace all and sundry. It is the 'charity', the 'Agape' described by St. Paul in Corinthians. At the lower level Neptune in aspect with Venus, especially in the seventh house, may indicate an unusual union, sometimes highly idealized, sometimes with a rather unreal quality about it. Or it may suggest a union in which the partner is weak, ill, or incapacitated or deformed, a union in which great sympathy is required if it is to survive. Alternatively it may suggest a Platonic affair, a union unconsummated on the one hand, or a succession of lovers taken and let go without discrimination or responsibility on the other.

Weak physical conditions. Lack of muscle tone. Tissue wasting. Flabbiness. Placcid forms of paralysis. Paresis. Paraesthesia. Paranormal sensation. Numbness. 'Phantom limb'. Neurasthenia. Trance. Coma. Unconsciousness. Nausea. Allergies. Hallucinations. Illusions. Confused mental states. Disorientation.

(From overleaf) In quantum physics Schroedinger's 'probability waves' are noticeably Neptunian in character. They indicate a tendency for something to happen - halfway between possibility and reality and recall Aristotle's concept of 'potentia'. The whole of astrology is based on this idea. Only in the last century has science caught up with it and demonstrated its existence in a form acceptable to subscribers to 'Nature' or other scientific journals. In chaos theory Neptune symbolises the all-embracing receptacle of chaos into which all order eventually falls and at the same time the womb of becoming out of whose chaos, order is again seen to arise.

Susceptibility to infection. Excess of tissue fluids. Oedema. Dropsy. Lower motor neurone paralysis. Infantile paralysis. People with Neptune prominent in their charts are often deep sleepers. They tend to an ambivalent attitude towards drugs and intoxicants. Either they too easily become addicts or they will have nothing to do with them and prefer to resort to natural therapies, homoeopathy and so on. Both Neptune and Uranus relate to tension. Within normal limits tension and relaxation relate to Mars and Venus respectively. High or abnormal tension, however, relates to Uranus, excessive relaxation, limpness, weakness to Neptune. Uranus and Neptune, indeed, are associated generally with everything that merits the prefix 'para-' such as paranoia and paradox (Uranus), paralysis and paraesthesia (Neptune), and of course parapsychology. In epilepsy Uranus (spasm) combines with Neptune (aura and coma).

PLUTO: Neutral. Somatotonic.

Pluto is associated with the sign Scorpio the eighth sign signifying death, and with Aries the first sign signifying new life or rebirth. It carries with it the idea of destruction and regeneration, transmutation, transformation, metamorphosis. The change, however, tends to be of a violent, eruptive nature. Pluto, otherwise known as Hades, was the god of the underworld and there is something of an underworld, underground nature in the picture presented by the astrological Pluto. The force of Pluto can be likened to the subterranean grumbling, seething eruptiveness of a volcano. Deeply buried complexes, repressed emotions, which may be brought to the surface and erupt in violent action are illustrative of the principle of Pluto. As co-ruler with Mars of the signs Aries and Scorpio Pluto is considered as a higher octave of Mars. With Pluto the inclination is to eliminate what is unwanted and to make a new start. It involves the urge to probe deep, to plumb the depths, both psychologically and materially. The desire to reform and refashion.

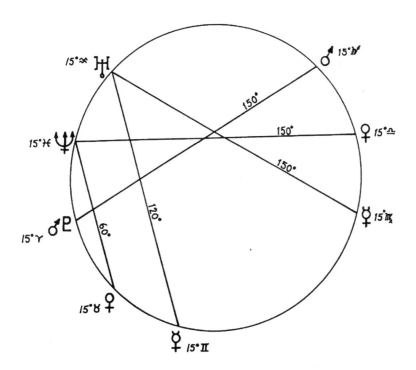

Figure 21 - HIGHER OCTAVE PLANETS

The relationship between personal planets and their impersonal 'higher octaves', i.e., Mercury - Uranus, Venus - Neptune and Mars - Pluto is shown in the accompanying diagram. The relationship is usually taken as one of simple affinity but as the diagram suggests there appears to be a deeper link with the zodiac itself.

Here Mercury - Uranus, Venus - Neptune and Mars - Pluto are linked by 150° aspects, while on the left of the circle we see Mercury - Uranus lined by a trine aspect, Venus - Neptune by a sextile and Mars - Pluto by a conjunction. The above suggests so far neglected links between Aquarius and Gemini or Virgo, and between Pisces and Taurus or Libra as well as the accepted one of Aries with Scorpio.

Repressed violence. Group violence. Violent eruptions. It symbolizes potential upheaval within the unconscious, an uprooting of buried complexes, as well as the probing analysis and penetration in depth necessary to accomplish it. It also relates to the deeper hidden springs of sexuality and, again in Scorpionic fashion, to death and rebirth. Pluto could perhaps be described as the 'pressure-cooker' of the psyche. Potentially explosive like Uranus the explosion, should it occur, is hidden and 'subterranean' rather than visible and in the open as with Uranus. Together with Uranus and Neptune, Pluto reflects the supernormal or subnormal. Individuals with one or more of these planets dominant in a horoscope are likely to be unusual or unconventional to some extent. They do not, however, play a big part unless in close aspect with the Ascendant, Midheaven, Sun or Moon.

Ulcers. Boils. Abscesses. Festering sores. Whitlows. The eliminating processes. Excretion. The elimination of toxins. The action of anti-bodies. Resistance to infection and disease. While the oxygen-carrying red cells of the blood relate to Mars, the white cells, the leucocytes, which protect the body against infection relate to Pluto. Leucocytosis. Phagocytosis. The failure of the auto-immune system. HIV. Aids.

CAPUT AND CAUDA DRACONIS: The Moon's North and South Nodes.

These are the points where the Moon's orbit crosses the Sun's path, the ecliptic. The union of the two paths symbolizes the capacity for forming associations, unions, alliances, societies, without any suggestion of emotional involvement as with Venus. Since Caput and Cauda are always 180 degrees apart it is only necessary to mark in Caput on the chart. The Moon's North Node is also extremely useful in timing events.

Each of the planetary pictures presented above relates a planet to a universal (Sun-like, Saturn-like) and also to a series of categories of meaning depending from the universal, even down, in some cases, to particulars. The meanings are not, of course, exhaustive and could be doubled or trebled without difficulty, but enough has been shown for the reader to get a good idea of the family to which each planetary symbol gives birth. Once this is recognized the reader can, as long as he keeps to the relevant categories, find an apposite meaning for any event.

We have, in the interests of space, restricted such descriptions and meanings largely to individual human beings and their physical and mental characteristics. They may, however, be equally applied to any event whatever, whether involving human beings or not. The horoscope is a diagram qualifying a moment in time at a certain place, colouring and giving meaning to it. When applied to the human subject it suggests a potential which he may or may not fulfil. But it could just as well be applied to an event such as a marriage, a dispute, the birth of a horse, the completion of a manuscript or whatever. A whole world of meaning is accommodated in the symbolism of astrology.

In the above attributions some curious affinities or analogies are evident, notably the connection of the characteristics of Uranus and Pluto with the explosive qualities of Uranium and Plutonium and their critical instability. Similarly the quality of ductility and conductivity associated with Venus is also possessed by its associated metal, copper, the reflective quality of the Moon is mirrored in its metal, silver, the weight and dullness of Saturn is reflected in its metal lead while mercurial changeability is recognizable in the metal Mercury, or quicksilver.[4]

It is idle to speculate which came first, the meaning or the substance. Like everything else in this world in which, we are now told, everything is interconnected and mutually supported, meaning and substance are 'intervolved'. What reason balks at, analogy and affinity bring to light. Ribot recognized this in his well-known essay on the creative imagination. It is now recognized that for radical new discovery in science one must go beyond reason. The part played by intuition, the 'Eureka experience', is well attested. Nevertheless intuition is not universally welcome among scientists; like teleology it is ostensibly black-balled and the model of the world put before us is predominantly a rational one.

The rational model is that symbolized by the planets Mercury and Saturn (reason and materialism), a model which while safe and reliable is also limited. But there is more to life than that which we can see, touch, count and analyze. The trans-Saturnian planets Uranus, Neptune and Pluto hint at something beyond what we take to be reality. Like the theory of relativity and quantum mechanics we are led into worlds so devoid of solid matter as to be virtually non-existent, figments of mind. At a higher level they suggest a world of values attained not by reason but by intuition (Uranus), enlightenment (Neptune) or regeneration (Pluto).

IX. HOUSES OF CONTENTION

'If a house be divided against itself, that house cannot stand.'

We have dealt in a previous chapter with the meanings of houses. We must now consider how houses fit into the horoscope and how they relate to the basic schema provided by the Meridian and Horizon. The area covered by a house is variable according to the system of house determination or 'domification' employed, so that a planet in the tenth house in one system may appear in the ninth or the eleventh in another. There is no meaningful rationale to this outside the mere process of calculation. Meaning is twisted without rational explanation to conform arbitrarily with the choice of system. There is no basic underlying structure of meaning to which everything may be referred. In what follows we advocate a system, ancient but neglected, which remedies this defect and can be universally applied, using as our example the chart of Albert Einstein.

To refresh the memories of readers we append the following tables of symbols:

Personal Factors ↓
- Asc. = Ascendant
- MC. = Midheaven
- ☉ = Sun
- ☽ = Moon
- ☿ = Mercury
- ♀ = Venus
- ♂ = Mars

Impersonal Factors ↓
- ♃ = Jupiter
- ♄ = Saturn
- ♅ = Uranus
- ♆ = Neptune
- ♇ = Pluto
- ☊ = Caput Draconis

- ♈ = Aries
- ♉ = Taurus
- ♊ = Gemini
- ♋ = Cancer
- ♌ = Leo
- ♍ = Virgo
- ♎ = Libra
- ♏ = Scorpio
- ♐ = Sagittarius
- ♑ = Capricorn
- ♒ = Aquarius
- ♓ = Pisces

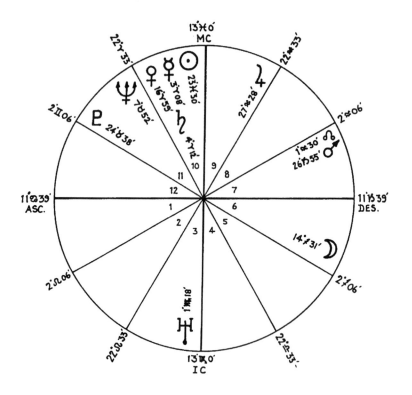

Figure 22 - Albert Einstein. b.14.3.1879. Ulm. Germany. 11.30 am.

The above is the conventional or popular type of horoscope. The four quadrants are each divided into three equal sections to form the houses - a system invented by Porphyry (AD 232-304) a follower of Plotinus. The question of house division has been a bone of contention for centuries and there are several different systems of which this is one of the simplest. The reader should not rely on any of them. Only the Meridian and Horizon are beyond argument. Their poles, the Ascendant and Descendant for the horizon, the Midheaven (MC) and Lower Heaven (IC) for the meridian are the most personal factors in any horoscope.

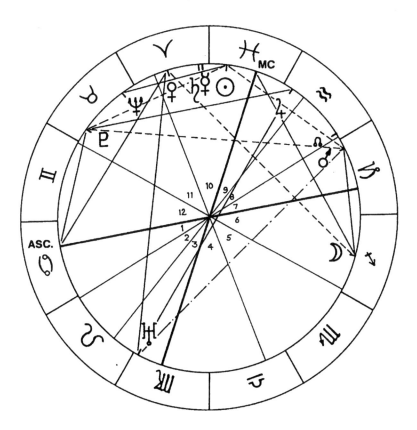

Figure 23 The above chart is drawn with the Zodiac as base-plate and the Meridian and Horizon occupying their respective degrees in the Zodiac. Opposite quadrants are divided into three equal sectors (after Porphyry). This chart enables aspects between planets to be clearly seen. Lines joining planets indicate oppositions, squares, semi- and sesquisquares. Interrupted lines indicate trines and sextiles. The aspects between Mars and Uranus is a bi-quintile (144°). A variation of this chart is used when comparing two or more horoscopes. In this case the Zodiac is always arranged with the sign Aries on the left, the sign Capricorn at the top. The Midheaven and Ascendant may then be found according to their zodiacal positions anywhere round the circle.

A third way of presenting a chart, and possibly the oldest, is that known as the Equal House System, first adopted by Ptolemy, author of that curious 'bible' of astrology 'The Tetrabiblos'. This consists of taking the Ascendant as the point from which to calculate and dividing the circle into equal sectors of thirty degrees. In this case the tenth house is always at exact right angles to the first and the cusp (the leading edge) of the tenth does symbolic duty as Derived Midheaven or 'Nonagesimal'. This is effective if the whole chart is seen in terms of the meanings of the Horizon, e.g., external, physical, immediate, spatial or environmental. The rationale here is that the symbolism and geometry of meaning is reflected in the structure based on the 'ideal' ninety degree difference between Ascendant and Meridian whatever the actual distance between the two.

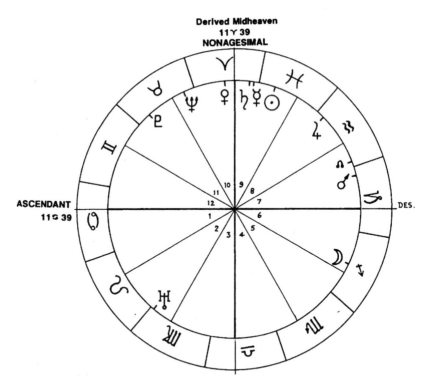

Figure 24

A complement to Equal House from the Ascendant is Equal House from the Midheaven. This system, or something close to it, was adopted by Morinus (Morin de Villefranche, mathematician and astrologer to Cardinal Richelieu). It should be read in terms of the meanings of the Meridian, e.g., internal, mental, teleological, temporal or hereditary - the individual 'within himself' in time rather than in relationship with others in space. Here we see the 'Derived Ascendant' in Gemini the sign of intellect and from a mental point of view this sign might well seem more appropriate as Ascendant than Cancer. Here the ruler Mercury is in the tenth house. Jupiter, ruler of the Midheaven is in the ninth with all its associations of higher learning (Whitehead's 'higher appetition') while the other ruler of the Midheaven (purpose, long term aims) Neptune is with Venus in the eleventh, the house of intellectual creativity or discovery. Uranus, the planet of discovery is in the mental third house.

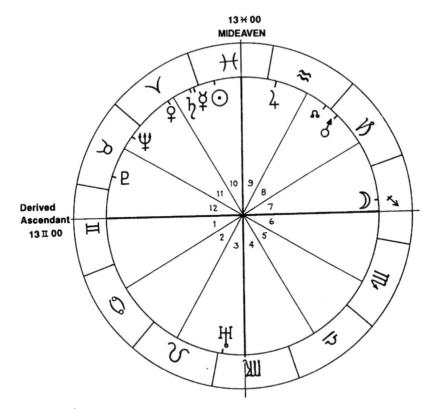

Figure 25[1]

Both the above systems were brought together some years ago by the Late Brigadier Firebrace, a former president of the Astrological Association, in a monograph entitled 'A and M Houses'. Unfortunately few astrologers appear to have profited from it. Nevertheless it provides a structure for balancing outer and inner experience, environment and heredity, means and ends. This balance is achieved in theory by finding the mid-point between the Ascendant and the Derived Ascendant, a point we will dub the Composite Ascendant, and between the Midheaven and the Derived Midheaven which we will call the Composite Midheaven. On these points a third Equal House System is erected. In Einstein's case it will be seen that if we compare the three charts the Composite chart has a closer accord with the Meridian based horoscope, i.e., with the mental aspect rather than the physical as befits a man whose life was dedicated to mental exertion of the most abstract, abstruse nature.

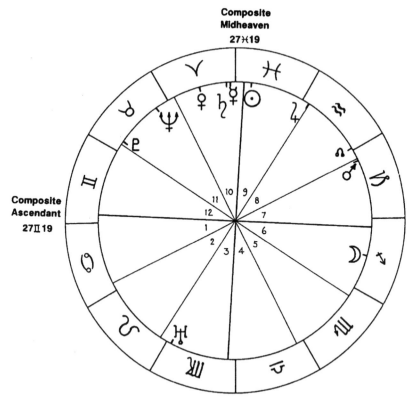

Figure 26

The advantage of Equal House systems is that, though purely symbolical, they maintain the geometry of meaning so implicit in the structure of astrology. No other systems do this and since they are all at odds with each other cannot be relied upon. We now have more than one way of looking at a horoscope. If the paramount interest is immediate, environmental and relates to outer experience or concerns the body rather than the mind, or the phenotype rather than the genotype, then the system based on the Horizon is relevant. If, on the other hand, the main interest concerns past or future, long term aims or ideals, purpose, inner experience, instinctive or hereditary factors, the genotype rather than the phenotype, the mind rather than the body, then the system based on the Meridian becomes relevant. If we wish to achieve some balance between the claims of one or other system then the Composite Chart becomes of use. We are back now with Ernst Cassirer's idea in The Philosophy of Symbolic Forms whereby ideas are seen to relate to this basic Meridian - Horizon cross which appears fundamental to the structure of thought.

It will be recognized that there are occasions when Meridian and Horizon are actually, as well as symbolically, at right angles to each other. This occurs twice a day when the Midheaven is at 0° Cancer and 0° Capricorn, or when the subject happens to be born on the Equator (0° of latitude). In such cases the claims of Meridian and Horizon are seen to relate to each other both actually and symbolically and one chart not only suffices but is indeed possible. One would expect an otherworldly man wrapt in abstraction and abstruse calculations to have the extra-Saturnian planets prominent if our astrological rationale makes any sense. Here we see the Sun sextile Pluto, semi-square Neptune and in 7°30' multiple aspect (actually 7°30' X 21) with Uranus. The Mid-point Uranus/Pluto aspects the Midheaven. The Mid-point Jupiter/Pluto is square the Ascendant. The Mid-point Jupiter/Uranus aspects the Moon. The Mid-point Neptune/Pluto aspects Uranus, and if we add Uranus 1°.18, Neptune 7°.52 and Pluto 24°.32 together and divide by three we get a triple Mid-point Uranus/Neptune/Pluto in 11°.14, aspecting the Ascendant. All the above aspects are well within one degree of exactitude with the exception of Sun sextile Pluto (1°.02'). Such multiple permutations are, of course, increasingly abstracted from reality. We no longer have our feet on the ground but are well up into Plato's *hyperouranios topos* or super celestial sphere. Nevertheless the symbolism fits, however remote and tortuous the process.

X. TEMPORAL CHANGE
Does the clock work?

Tempora mutantur et nos mutamur in illis
Astra regunt homines, sed regit astra Deus.
(Times change and we change with them.
The stars rule men, but God rules the stars).

Admirable parenté mathématique des hommes.
Que dire de cette forêt de relations et de correspondances?[1]

(Valéry)

We have dealt with astrology as a system for co-ordination and relating ideas but we have not dealt with it in time. In other words we have studied the clock but have not wound it up to see whether it works. In order to do this we have to make use of 'transits' (the actual positions of planets in the heavens at a moment in time) and also of symbolic systems of progression by which sun, moon and planets are considered to move at a symbolic rate correlating with the difference in time between the date of birth of the subject and the event to be examined. This latter is usually achieved in two ways. The first is the simplest and consists in adding to all the birth planets a measure called the Sun-arc. This is reckoned according to the theory that one year of life may correspond to one day. According to this measure the Sun actually moves about one degree a year - a little more or a little less according to the time of year - on average it moves 0°58' per year (a measure known as the Naibod arc after Valentin Naibod, 1510-1593, a professor of mathematics at Cologne and Padua). The actual Sun-arc however can be discovered by referring to an ephemeris of planetary positions for the period in question. Lacking an ephemeris, the Naibod arc is a workable approximation. The Sun-arc measure is applied not only to planets but to Midheaven and Ascendant as well.

The second way is to find the relevant position of the Sun by Sun-arc in the ephemeris and then read from the ephemeris the planetary positions for that day. The second method is a step nearer reality than the first in that it reflects, though at reduced speed (one three hundred and sixty-fifth) the actual movement of the planets. By this method, however, the remoter planets may scarcely move at all. The first method is known as 'Directions', the second as 'Progressions'.[2]

A horoscope develops with time, the sun, moon and planets circling the heavens and taking up positions which may relate, by aspect, to the original birth positions. Where there is a relationship, for instance, between the progressed or directed Saturn at any time and the birth position of the subject's Sun then this is considered to be a period when the subject may experience increased responsibility, frustration, authority, restriction or any other meaning attributable to the symbolism of Saturn.

Another system is known as the Solar Return. This involves setting up a chart for the moment when the Sun returns to the exact degree and minute that it occupied at birth and re-occurs around each birthday, within a day or two. It is considered to be valid for the year in question and to suggest, when related to the birth chart, the potentialities for the subject for that period. In the accompanying chart for 1915, the year of the General Theory of Relativity the zodiac circle has been set up with Aries on the left so that the Ascendant and Midheaven are not in their accustomed positions on the page, but of course their positions within the zodiac remain unchanged.

In the chart below the planet Neptune is emphasized. It is conjunct the Descendant and trine both Sun and MC, and together with the Ascendant forms a perfect 'kite' formation. This brings all four into a combination of meaning and since the aspects are trines and sextiles, a favourable one. If the MC is interpreted as 'purpose' or 'aim' then it is furthered by the Sun principle (enterprise, creative power) and by Neptune (idealism, abstraction, limitless space). The ruler of the Ascendant, Saturn, is conjunct the ruler of the Midheaven, Pluto, both being situated in the fifth house, the house of creativity. This indicates a conjunction of means and ends in the work of creation. The MC is in exact opposition to the natal Pluto suggesting radical change or transformation while the return Pluto re-emphasizes this with its bi-quintile aspect (144°) to the MC, (dotted line in the chart). Mercury is conjunct the natal Jupiter and both form a mid-point for Jupiter/Uranus which could be interpreted as a fortunate (Jupiter) combination of reason (Mercury) with intuition (Uranus). Uranus itself is in semi-sextile aspect with the natal MC and sextile natal Moon. Most significantly the return Jupiter/Uranus/Pluto mid-point (fortunate, sudden radical transformation, or, according to the Combination of Stellar

Influences 'the attainment of immense success') is in exact aspect with the natal Neptune (to the minute).

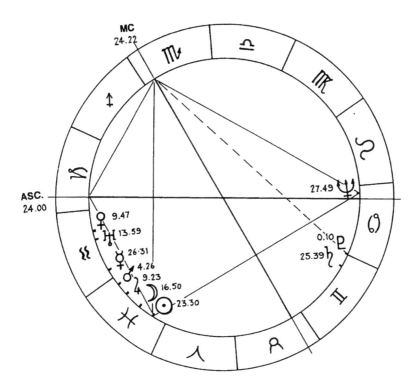

Figure 27 - Einstein: Solar return for 1915, the year of the General Theory of Relativity.

A useful adjunct to the horoscope is the Thirty Degree Chart.³ In this the 360° of the normal circle is, as it were, contracted into 30° as if the twelve signs of the zodiac were contracted into one. Planets are inserted in this chart solely according to their sign degree so that a planet in 12° Taurus, one in 12° Gemini and one in 12° Leo would all occupy the same place. The advantage of this is that aspects are readily discernible, even those of 15° and their multiples, and further, those of 7°30' and their multiples. These latter aspects, most of which are neglectable in the birth chart, come into their own when events in time come to be symbolized and orbs of aspects out to, say, one degree. The chart is also convenient for siting relevant midpoints. All degrees in conjunction or opposition across the circle are in 0° or 15° multiple aspect. Those in square are in 7°30' or 7°30' multiple aspect. Again Einstein's birth chart is the example.

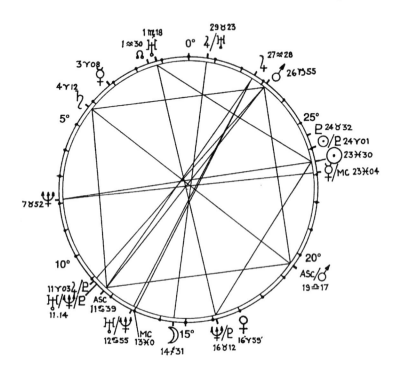

Figure 28

We will not pursue the matter of 'progressions'. This is not a textbook for astrologers, nevertheless a quick look at 'directions' may be helpful to readers. The Sun-arc for Einstein's 36th birthday, the year of the General Theory, is 36°09'. If we add this to the natal Uranus we find that it comes to an aspect with Neptune. If we add it to Neptune it then makes an aspect to the Moon. If we add 36°09' to Pluto it aspects Uranus and if we add it to the Sun we find Sun aspecting Jupiter/Uranus while adding it to Jupiter brings it into contact with Mercury. All the above aspects are within one degree of exactitude and it is noteworthy that 36 degrees is a semi-quintile aspect, but perhaps the most surprising feature is that if we add 36°09' to the natal Ascendant we find the directed Ascendant aspecting the natal Jupiter/Uranus/Pluto to the exact minute. Again if we take the natal Jupiter/Uranus/Pluto and add the Sun-arc to it we find it comes to an aspect with the Sun.

On the 18th November 1915 Einstein received the news that an experiment concerning the precession of Mercury had verified his General Theory which up till then had not been confirmed. He was overjoyed - 'For a few days I was beside myself with joyous excitement'. On that day the Sun was at 25°07' Scorpio opposing natal Pluto. Jupiter, Pluto and Neptune were aspecting natal Mercury. Uranus was aspecting natal Asc/MC. Most significantly, however, the natal Ascendant was aspected by the transiting midpoint Jupiter/Uranus/Pluto. Here again the contacts are within one degree of exactitude. Significantly the combination Jupiter/Uranus/Pluto is prominently figured in the Solar Return, in the Directions, and also in the Event Chart for 18th November. 'The attainment of immense success'.

Further confirmation of the General Theory came on the 29th May 1919 when Eddington, who had been watching the eclipse of the sun on that date, noted that during the eclipse the transmission of light was bent thus verifying Einstein's calculations from another angle. On that date Sun and Moon were in conjunction in the seventh degree of Gemini, sextile Neptune in 7°00' Leo, all three aspecting Einstein's natal Neptune. Uranus was in exact opposition to the natal Uranus (within half a degree), Jupiter was in 16°00' Cancer aspecting both the natal and the transit Uranus. Pluto was in 5°25' Cancer aspecting the natal MC by 7°30', all the above contacts being again well within one degree. is the combination Jupiter/Uranus/Pluto in significant aspect here too? Yes it is. It falls in 7°41' aspecting natal Neptune and the eclipse position of Sun, Moon, Neptune and, by 15° multiple aspect, also Mercury and Saturn, all again within one degree and all focused on Einstein's natal Neptune, a truly remarkable configuration.

Another instance of radical discovery is that of the DNA 'Double Helix'. Here the Jupiter/Uranus/Pluto complex on the day of the discovery (28.2.1953 in Cambridge) is in aspect with Watson's natal Jupiter and Crick's natal Sun, both of whom won the Nobel Prize for their efforts. We will not go further into this event; we have already expatiated at length on Einstein, but for those who might like to experiment planetary positions are as follows: **Crick:** Sun 17°20' Gemini, Moon 11°36' Virgo, Mercury 13°39' Gemini, Venus 19°27' Cancer, Mars 5°14' Virgo, Jupiter 26°51' Aries, Saturn 15°46' Cancer, Uranus 19°37' Aquarius, Neptune 0°47' Leo, Pluto 2°25' Cancer (timed for mid-day 8th June 1916, as exact time of birth unknown). **Watson:** Asc. 14°12' Capricorn, MC. 9°50' Scorpio, Sun 16°15' Aries, Moon 28°53' Libra, Mercury 22°36' Pisces, Venus 23°33' Pisces, Mars 29°01' Aquarius, Jupiter 16°29' Aries, Saturn 19°04' Sagittarius, Uranus 4°06' Aries, Neptune 26°39' Leo, Pluto 15°00' Cancer. (1.23am CST, 6 April 1928, Chicago; birth certificate.) **DNA Discovery:** Sun 9°32' Pisces, Moon 5°28' Virgo, Mercury 27°27' Pisces, Venus 22°40' Aries, Mars 14°58' Aries, Jupiter 15°34' Taurus, Saturn 26 50' Libra, Uranus 14 39' Cancer, Neptune 23°34' Libra, Pluto 21°36' Leo.

From the above it would seem that the Zeitgeist was operating true to form. But, of course, there were others born on the same day and at the same time as Einstein was, or Crick or Watson. It has been estimated that something like two people in five million have approximately the same horoscope, i.e., something in the neighbourhood of forty in Germany alone. What, one wonders, occurred to those others on the 18th November 1915. The answer is not necessarily anything very much, or indeed anything at all, for we must not forget that we are dealing with potentialities and those are not always, indeed rather rarely, realized. Einstein realized his, or rather the experiment concerning the eccentricities of Mercury's orbit realized it for him and confirmed his theory. It could be that others of his contemporaries also realized their potential but planetary symbolism as a vehicle for concepts allows considerable latitude for interpretation and the planet Uranus, for instance, as indeed all others, has a multitude of associated meanings. All we can say is that if something did materialize to a contemporary its character would conform *in some way* with the symbolism of the moment.

XI. PROOF

'The demand for scientific objectivity makes it inevitable that every scientific statement must remain tentative for ever'.

Karl Popper

To the materialist scientist and rationalist academic astrology is nonsense, not because he has studied it and found it wanting but because his beliefs exclude the possibility of astrology being anything but nonsense. His beliefs, therefore, preclude him from any such study. Why waste time doing so when by his standards it cannot be true, and of course if one restricts one's beliefs to the lowest common denominator of what can be measured and logically demonstrated then there is no point in looking further. Astrology is happily dismissed to the realm of the occult and women's magazines and should never be permitted to emerge from there. After all that is the only sort of astrology he has encountered. There it presents no threat and there he is happy to keep it, while the performance of popular astrology does much to confirm his antipathy.

Nevertheless there have been serious attempts to prove or disprove astrology. A few years ago there were two which reached the general public. The first was by a statistician, Dr. Michel Gauquelin, who after examining the birth data of thousands of notable people in the professions, together with sportsmen and military men, came to the conclusion that there was undoubtedly a correlation between achievement and planetary position but that it did not relate, except peripherally, to traditional astrology. The second attempt, conducted by the psychologist Professor Hans Eysenck, was inconclusive.

One reason why the writer is sceptical of attempts to prove or disprove astrology is that its structure is an integrated 'Gestalt', a pattern of meaning wherein the parts cannot be properly understood in isolation without relation to the whole.† Reductionist investigation which singles out one or more features from the whole is a form of distortion.[1] It also involves subjective selectivity, not only in method but also in interpretation. It is all very well to use a computer but what is fed into the computer is both selective and

---

† 'Modern physics has taught us that the nature of any system cannot be discovered by dividing it into its component parts and studying each part itself.... We must keep our attention fixed on the whole and on the inter-connection between the parts.' (Max Planck: 'The Philosophy of Physics', London, 1936)

subjective. Moreover the question of potentiality and actuality which might be presumed to be catered for by the statistical method is not really adequately addressed at all. Potentiality in astrology is paralleled in quantum theory and more particularly in the experiment known as 'Schroedinger's Cat', in which the cat is neither alive nor dead but in a state of 'limbo' or suspension, i.e., potentiality, and is only brought to life, or death, by the action of an observer. Potentiality is an integral part of astrology as we have taken pains to establish. Everything is in limbo, like Kant's 'noumenon', in suspension, for possible but not necessary, actualization. Critics do not seem to appreciate this. They are shadow-boxing without even a vestige of a shadow or, as H.G. Wells put it, in another context, 'trying to shoot the square root of two with a rook rifle'.

Let us then say with Popper that everything must remain tentative; but that does not mean that further enquiry is futile. Reductionism is *convergent thinking*, narrowing down possibilities to achieve an answer which is, as likely as not, taken as certainty. It is permissible to use convergent thinking as long as one recognizes its limitations. One can learn perhaps something from astrology, bit by bit, but it is a fragmented picture and a skewed one. Unlike the conventions of orthodox science astrology is open-ended, an instrument of *divergent thinking*, even a system which makes provision for 'lateral thinking', or 'la pensée à côté' as Souriau calls it, in the last two signs and the planets Uranus and Neptune. This heuristic aspect is an important one as we have seen in the chart of Albert Einstein. Failing certainty, astrology should be employed as a working hypothesis.

One of the more convincing approaches to accepting astrology as a working hypothesis is a study of the horoscopes of families, for generations. The British royal family is an excellent example. Times of birth are all meticulously recorded and the dates of events affecting them, marriages, deaths, divorces and so on are available to anyone. When one sees the same degrees coming up again and again, from horoscope to horoscope, one cannot avoid the thought that an astrological link is very likely. To take just two examples, and there are many others, the Queen's Sun and Prince Charles' Moon occupy the same degree of Taurus. Prince Philip's Ascendant and Prince Charles' Ascendant occupy the same degree of Leo.

Another avenue of approach is the comparison of coincident birthdates of unrelated persons. Such birthdates not infrequently tally with coincident professions. An article published by J.M. Addey in the Astrological Journal, Vol. IX, No. 1.1966, gives the following incidences: Pablo Casals and Lionel Tertis (both 29.12.1876), one a world-famous exponent of the cello, the other a well-known virtuoso on the viola, the tenors Lauritz Melchior and Beniamino Gigli (both 20.3.1890), the Irish writers James Joyce and James Stephens (2.2.1882), the writers Emerson and Bulwer Lytton (8.11.1831), the inventors Sir John Boyd Dunlop and Sir Hiram Maxim (5.2.1840) and the distinguished surgeons Sir John Broadbent and Sir Comyns Berkeley (16.10.1865). This last pair is a particularly interesting instance as both were married at the age of twenty-nine within a few weeks of each other and at the same church, and both died on the same day - 27 January 1946. We can multiply such coincidences many times, and indeed there are countless such instances, but they would still not provide proof. Nevertheless they do suggest that our working hypothesis is working rather more efficiently than we might have credited.

Coincident birthdates of unrelated people born on the same day of the same year are one thing. Coincident birthdates of related people born in different years are quite another. The record for the latter is surely held by Ralph and Carolyn Cummins of Clintwood, Virginia, U.S.A. The Guiness Book of Records states that their five children were all born on 20 February as follows: Catherine 20.2.1952, Carol 20.2.1953, Charles 20.2.1956, Claudia 20.2.1961 and Cecilia 20.2.1966. The book records that the odds against this happening are 17,797,577,730, i.e., almost four times the world's population.

We realize that we will never dent the armour of those determined never to shed it, but to the uncommitted, the enquiring and the open-minded there is surely here food for thought. In astrology time, place and event come together in significant coincidence, a coincidence which can be geometrically plotted and explicitly interpreted. It relates the individual to his world as if sewn into it, or participating ('methexis') in it, and conversely, a view in keeping not only with the geometry of Plato in the Timaeus but with post-atomic physics and philosophy since Kant.

Prejudice, however, is a mind-set difficult to overcome and prejudice is as common among scientists as it is among other disciplines or social groups. When Einstein published his theory of relativity scientists in Germany set up societies to oppose it, reminding one of the action of the Catholic Church against Galileo. As Wilfred Trotter remarked: 'The mind likes a strange idea as little as the body likes a strange protein and resists it with a similar energy. It would not perhaps be too fanciful to say that a new idea is the most quickly acting antigen known to science. If we watch ourselves honestly we shall often find that we have begun to argue against a new idea even before it has been completely stated'. Astrology is such a 'strange protein' and the body of orthodox opinion will no doubt continue to reject it. This is a formidable obstacle to new discovery but happily not a fatal one. There will always be a few bold enough to break the rules as science itself testifies in such eccentrics as Einstein, Planck, Heisenberg, Schroedinger, Pauli and others. It was indeed Niels Bohr who said to Wolfgang Pauli that the only thing that worried him was that he doubted whether Pauli's theory was crazy enough to have any chance of being correct.

XII. END PIECE

We have attempted to demonstrate a rationale for a subject commonly believed to be irrational. We will illustrate just one more instance where reason, symbol and structure come together to present us with a picture which we can accept as valid. To anyone of an inquiring mind who first comes upon astrology the question must cross his or her mind - why is the Ascendant considered the most important factor in the whole horoscope, why not, for instance, the Descendant? According to the laws of physics action and reaction are equal and opposite. They are supposed to balance and complement each other, why the preference for the Ascendant? There is no obvious reason why one pole should be preferred to the other - until we look at their respective meanings.

The Ascendant represents subjectivity, the ego, spontaneity, natural impulse, self interest and inequality, in other words those primitive characteristics which we defensively exculpate with such words as 'It's only human nature'. The Descendant, on the other hand, implies at least a modicum of objectivity (complete objectivity is a chimera), consideration, altruism and equality. In view of the violent, bloodthirsty history of mankind it cannot, surely, be denied that the former qualities have been much more in evidence than the latter. Our newspapers and new bulletins are sorry testimony to the interest and appetite the former qualities engender. Ascendant and Descendant values are equal but in our imperfect world they are not considered to be so. The first instinct of any child is 'me first'. Its complement 'others too', though recognized as an ideal by parents and teachers does not come naturally, or without a struggle, to the child. The same can be said of interested groups, firms and even nations. Laissez faire capitalism could scarcely survive without the values attributed to the Ascendant. Instead of co-operation, equality, help and care for others, mankind has preferred competition, inequality, disregard for others, domination and war. At least this appears to be true for the male half of the population. Aristophanes' 'Lysistrata' was written around the problem of male aggression, and it is as rife now as it was then. The symbolism is emphasized by Mars as the planet associated with the Ascendant. Moreover we live in a world in which male values are predominant everywhere.

The qualities ascribed to the Ascendant come naturally to us. We do not stop to think or weigh things up - we act. The qualities ascribed to the Descendant come, not spontaneously or readily, but often with difficulty. We think before we act and our action may well require some personal sacrifice or consideration for others. Cooperation is one instance of this and co-operation does not come easily - the 'harmony in contrariety' is not to be had for the asking, nor is the moderating of primitive instinct. Equality now raises its head cautiously above the parapet and becomes of importance. Sexual equality especially is a female, not a male aim. This is symbolized by Venus as the planet associated with the Descendant and, as we have seen in the list of planetary qualities, Venus is the planet of balance. The answer, in astrology, to the imbalance of male dominance is through the dialectic in which male aggression is embraced, softened and transformed by the female qualities of the Descendant, just as in coition male virility and rigidity soon succumb and become slack and tranquil within the physical embrace of the female. This coniunctio oppositorum echoes Karl Popper's claim that animal behaviour and structure are biological analogues of mental constructions which in turn correspond to bodily organs in their method and function.

It will be seen from the above that body, symbol and meaning reflect each other not only in structure and function but also in planetary significance confirming once again the link between our world as represented in the horoscope and our minds and bodies. However, each house and sign, not just the Ascendant and Descendant, may be subjected to similar interpretation, suggesting that if Kepler was wrong in his idea that 'the soul bears within itself the idea of the zodiac' he was, nevertheless, broadly and in essence not far wrong. Once again we hear echoes of the basic ideas of Plato and the Pythagoreans. That astrology can also be seen to relate to the ideas of Kant, Hegel and others could be further confirmation that meaning and apparent world structure are strangely, but profoundly interconnected, just as now sub-atomic physics suggests, in similar vein, that we and our world are one.

Another question arises. How did those who first dreamed up the concept of astrology work it all out? Did they reason it out empirically from observation of the heavens matched with studies of the vagaries of human nature? Did they intuit it? Was it some 'divine inspiration' or 'revelation'? Or was it all there already, innate, *a priori*, structured into the human mind as, indeed, we have suggested in the case of mathematics, an idea foreshadowed in Plato's Meno where Socrates claims that knowledge is essentially a question of re-call (Gk. anamnesis). It is noteworthy that astrology in some form or another has, at one time or another, formed a part of the world view of all civilized peoples. If we discount illogical answers and restrict ourselves to the empirical and rational ('anamnesic') solutions we find ourselves once again transfixed on the horns of a dilemma, a dualism which invades every particular at the moment of its manifestation. If, however, we mount the scale of 'becoming' from particular to universal we see that the two, once again, are but complementary aspects of the one. If we include the irrational we then have intuition versus reason, again a dualism inviting a similar resolution. The truth, surely, lies once again in the coniunctio oppositorum, the 'harmony in contrariety'. The simple truth rests on a coming together of half-truths, where a half-truth is not an untruth but a true half of a whole truth.

At the beginning of this book we attempted to take a philosophical look at astrology. We need now to take an astrological view of philosophy. The philosophy of Kant, Hegel, Russell and others rests necessarily on logic and on that level we can move, step by step, through close argument to a view of the world which seems to us reasonable, if perhaps rather dry, spare and skeletal. But the world presented to us by them is a limited one and arises out of ratiocination rather than out of experience. Like the world of science it is constantly changing - from Descartes to Kant was a big step - and it will go on changing. Moreover it has no aim but to explain.

Astrology, however, though logical in construction, provides us in its symbolism with further vistas of conceptual thought not tied to the restrictive exigencies of logic or the accepted 'facts' of a science which, for all its achievements, is limited and liable to have its findings confuted by succeeding generations. Unlike logic or science there are no 'certainties' to vanish with time, only suggestions, hypotheses, associations of ideas and heuristic combinations. It is 'open-ended' and adds to cold reason, 'bloodless categories' and colourless empiricism the warmth of imagination and the prospect of unpredictable discovery.

In his representation of astrology in the Timaeus Plato's aim was the *megiston mathema*, the highest knowledge - 'The Good'. The Good, however, is not the result of reasoning but of personal discovery, intuition or enlightenment. Reason can take us so far but then the mind has to take a leap into the unknown. the 'Eureka experience', the blinding flash of intuition on the road to Damascus has its representation in the symbolism of the planet Uranus, the subsequent 'enlightenment' relates to Neptune, and the 'conversion' or 'regeneration' to Pluto, all planets associated with the unconscious, the sub-liminal mind, or perhaps the collective unconscious. Here we are beyond reason into the 'Cloud of Unknowing', 'The Dark Night of the Soul', and lightening intuition. As Paul Valéry has pointed out with regard to the Eureka experience, radical discovery is not the child of reason. Disorder and dung are good breeding grounds; order and sterile conditions kill the germ of an idea at birth. Great discoveries arise unbidden from the subconscious disorder of our minds, not from our reason. Astrology goes beyond reason in associations with the unconscious and sub-liminal mind represented by the three trans-Saturnian planets. Its heuristic aspect, moreover, is not confined to physical or theoretical discovery but presents us with a beacon in the poorly charted seas of ethics. Here the aim is the megiston mathema, the Good itself - the star in the heavens by which we steer our frail vessel, the longing within us which we do our best to stifle.

We are straying into forbidden territory, that of ethics. In our consideration of the Meridian we have discussed it as an index of time. But there is another dimension in which this diameter is relevant - the moral dimension. This is outside time. 'There is no time like the present' becomes there is no time but the present. Past and future have no existence but in the present; they never have had and never will have. But we act as though we can put the present right, not now but in the future. This leads us to pursuing 'isms', utopias which become soul destroying régimes, capitalisms which make the undeserving rich, and the poor even poorer than they were before, communisms which oppress and strait-jacket everyone in the name of 'power to the people', fascisms which brutalize and torture dissidents and indulge in pogroms and genocide, nationalisms which set one state against another and feed the dogs of war. We think we can set things right in the future but our pet utopia turns sour and becomes a prison camp, an avaricious, selfish free-for-all in which the weakest go to the wall, or a nation at war in which the poor, as ever, are made to suffer the arrogance not only of the instigators of the war but also of their own leaders. At its silliest extreme we put our trust in star wars and nuclear threats, all, of course, for the ultimate benefit of mankind, forgetting that there is no ultimate; there is only now. This is the result, in Aldous Huxley's words, of 'an overvaluation of happenings in time and an undervaluation of the everlasting, timeless fact of eternity'.

Astrology provides us with a structure for this dimension, this time not within passing time but within the eternal moment. We have to imagine the Meridian here as not lying flat on the page but as rising vertically from it. This takes us out of the succession of time and confines us to the present moment. We have now an internal hierarchical ladder - a scale of better or worse - instead of future and past, an individual scale of ethics. In this sense Meridian and Horizon come together and time is annihilated in the present. Our utopia is no longer in the future, it is now. We act now as if each act were our last. No more elimination of the Kulaks or construction of Gulags for a better communism in the future. No more pogroms or holocausts of Jews for the ultimate perfection of the 'master race'. No more sacrifice of the poor on the altar of the future economic millennium. No more genuflections to the bitch-goddess Progress. No more perversion of means for the perfection of ends, for means determine ends and ends do not exist except in our imagination. The message of astrology is we must make our means our ends. Our 'promised land' is now, what we make of it now, not in the future, for if we set it in the future we will pervert the present for the sake of it and the present is all we have, and all we will have.

This vertical scale of ethics is the axis of a different sort of philosophy, the Philosophia Perennis or Perennial Philosophy. Unlike other philosophies which change with time, this does not change. Over the centuries its upholders have consistently said the same things. In Aldous Huxley's eponymous book written nearly fifty years ago there are scores of examples of sayings of poets and mystics from many countries over the centuries. They insist that there is a 'divine ground' to everything and that man's end and purpose is to unite with this.

The geometry of the horoscope provides us with a structure illustrating such a timeless philosophy. The vertical ethical axis pierces the centre of the circle representing 'The Void', 'The Tao', 'Nirvana', 'The Divine Ground' or 'Godhead' which is also the original, ultimate and universal 'Idea'. The centre of the circle lies at the junction of three axes, those of Space, Time and Ethics, at the spot where Space-Time is annihilated. If the perimeter of the circle represents the body and, by extension, the world, the centre stands for the soul, spirit or Tao from which all originates and to which all returns. There is a spiralling outward from centre to perimeter and a spiralling inward from perimeter to centre, both physically and mentally. In the language of Hegel centre and perimeter are opposite and complementary. In the 'harmony in contrariety' the two come together. The 'All' and the 'Nothing', the 'Every Thing' and the 'No Thing', are one, however much, as denizens of Plato's 'Cave', we may see them as two.† Enlightenment is achieved in the Eureka experience (Uranus) and in Meditation (Neptune). In the Buddhist religion the former is attained by the Zen 'Koan', a typically Uranian phenomenon. In Christianity enlightenment is reached through meditation and prayer, the 'Dark Night of the Soul' (Neptune). In both we have the idea of re-birth and resurrection (Pluto).

In the geometry of the Platonic Dodecagon and its relations, the Golden Section, the Spira Mirabilis and the mathematics of the Fibonacci Series we begin to see how the structure of mind reflects that of nature, not precisely but loosely and suggestively. The other Platonic Solids, the Tetrahedron, Hexahedron, Octahedron and Icosahedron relate not only to the Elements, Sun, Earth, Air and Rain but also to their equivalent qualities of temperament as well as to states of matter - solid (Earth), liquid (Water, gaseous (Air) and electric (Fire). Though these are merely vehicles for concepts they provide us with symbols and sets of co-ordinates, categories of meaning which we can advantageously make use of in interpreting events and confirming our suppositions.

We have been attempting to relate astrology to aspects of philosophy. But philosophy is not life; it is an attempt through logical structure to provide tools with which we can examine life, and laws which we can apply to it. Logic, however, is a sharp weapon and life a vulnerable and elusive prey. The living subject is distorted by the unbending instrument we use to grasp it and the unrelenting laws with which we endeavour, in Procrustean manner,

---

† The concept of the identity of opposites is at least three thousand years old. It appears in the Upanishads and it influenced the thinking of Parmenides, Plato, Plotinus and Spinoza. Hegel was the first to state it in explicit terms but Eckhart anticipated both Spinoza and Hegel in subscribing to its influence. The idea of no distinction between subject and object is one of the bases of mysticism. (See W.T. Stace: 'Mysticism and Philosophy', Macmillan)

to cut it down to size. This is not to say, of course, that such instruments are useless, such laws futile, but they must be handled circumspectly and interpreted loosely. A lucid and arresting exposition of how life in all its manifestations cannot be pinned down and dissected by the sciences is that set out in Fritz Schumacher's 'A Guide for the Perplexed', and anyone who wants to understand astrology, though it is not about astrology, might benefit from reading it. The advantage of astrology is that, unlike the rigorous disciplines of philosophy and science, it merely suggests an avenue to explore, a potentiality that may possibly materialize, an unexpected or fruitful analogy and, in its symbolism, a prolific 'vehicle for concepts'. It provides us with a systematic, highly integrated, working hypothesis - a theory of potentiality. The French physiologist Claude Bernard once said, 'Theories are not true or false; they are fertile or sterile'. In the experience of the writer astrology is eminently fertile.

A last thought. We have been talking for much of the time as if the phenomenal world, the world that appears to us, is all that there is. But this world is limited, defined by our minds and by our sensory-motor equipment adapted to perceive it. It is odd that we do not consider that our minds and senses may be just as much blinkers or blind-folds as they are spectacles, telescopes and microscopes. They limit our perception as much as they enable us to see at all.[†] Who is to say that the cosmos does not contain many worlds, interpenetrating and woven into the cosmic 'arrangement'. When I read Stephen Hawking's 'Brief History of Time' I could not help thinking how limited such a brief history was and that Hawking apparently seemed unaware of it. A telescope may enable us to see a long way but it is only of use when pressed to an eye and that eye itself is limited to its apparent function, to relate what it sees to ourselves as human beings. What it does not see, because it cannot, is the whole cosmos itself. It selects out from the whole what is necessary for our existence, our world, and we obediently take the part for the whole. 'There are more things in heaven and earth, Horatio, than are dreamt of in your philosophy'.

[†] 'Das physikalische Weltbild hat nicht Unrecht mit dem, was es behauptet, sondern mit dem, was es verschweigt'. (Freiherr, von Weizsäcker: 'Zum Weltbild der Physik'). (The physical world-picture is not false in what it maintains but only in what it is silent about).

If we are ever to penetrate beyond the limits of the world presented to us by our minds and senses it will not be by means of science for science is tethered to the puny equipment conceded to that microscopic aberration of the cosmos - ourselves, pin-points in creation. How presumptuous to think that we know the answer when we have not yet apparently understood the question. The answer, if there is one, is beyond reason. In the words of Neils Bohr it must by crazy enough to be true. Is it not, therefore, just possible that astrology with its provision for the 'irrational' might prove a better instrument for understanding the cosmos and dispersing the 'cloud of unknowing'. We repeat 'just possible' and re-echo Karl Popper's 'tentative forever'. Astrology is still in its infancy, kept there as a delinquent child and dismissed as such, but there is where a wealth of heuristic potentiality which, taken seriously, may yet surprise us. The first and last injunction, however, is to keep an open mind.

NOTES

Introduction

1. (p. 3) Dane Rudhyar: 'The Astrology of Personality' (Servire, The Hague, 1963).

2. (p. 3) Thomas Ring: 'Astrologische Menschenkunde' (Rascher Verlag, Zurich, 1959).

3. (p. 3) Dr. Freiherr von Klöckler: 'Grundlagen für die Astrologische Deutung' and 'Astrologie als Erfahrungswissenschaft (H.F. Timm, Berlin, 1952, and Leipzig, 1957).

4. (p. 6) Universals are abstract properties, qualities and relations. In astrology they are represented by planetary symbols, zodiacal signs and the poles of Meridian and Horizon. Particulars are concrete 'things' that exemplify them. The Sun, for instance, as a thing is a particular; as an astrological symbol it is a universal - 'sun-like', and may relate to any particular which has sun-like qualities, e.g., light, brightness, warmth, radiation, vitality, etc., a fire, for instance, is a particular of which sun-like is the universal.

Chapter 1   Symbols and Participation

1. (p. 7) Cassirer uses the phrase 'animal symbolicum' for man.

2. (p. 7) One of Copernicus' instructors, Domenico Novaro, Professor of Mathematics and Astronomy at Bologna was a Pythagorean believing in the simplicity of harmony of the universe. He encouraged Copernicus to study the classics in order to discover the objections to the concept that the earth was immovable and the centre of the universe. He found that in the fifth century BC Hicetas, and two hundred years later Aristarchus, both taught the rotation of the earth in 24 hours, while the latter added that it was not the earth but the sun that was at the centre.

3. (p. 8) Gestalt - an organized pattern in which the qualities of the whole differ from those of the components of the pattern. The nature of the parts is determined by the whole and secondary to it.

4. (p. 8) Potentiality suggests a tendency. At atomic and sub-atomic level matter does not exist at a certain place but merely shows tendencies to exist. In quantum theory such tendencies appear as 'probability waves'. Sub-atomic particles inhabit a sort of limbo between existence and non-existence. It is impossible to separate a perceived object from the mind of the perceiver, since together they constitute a single, integral reality. This applies also to astrology where the potential suggested by the symbolism is only realized by the observation of an actual event.

5. (p. 8) 'From the very outset Plato searched for the supreme authority, knowledge of which first lends meaning to thought and action. He calls it the highest science (megiston mathema). To attain it, no effort is too great.' (Karl Jaspers: 'The Great Philosophers', ed. Hannah Arendt).

6. (p. 9) Whitehead - mathematician and Platonist philosopher, tutor of Bertrand Russell at Cambridge. Collaborated with Russell in 'Principia Mathematica'. Author among other works of 'Science in the Modern World', 'Adventures of Ideas' and 'Process and Reality'.

7. (p. 12) 'The moon by reason of its spectacular changes, is a very expressive, adaptable and striking symbol - far more than the sun, with its simple career and unvarying form. A little contemplation shows quite clearly why the moon is so apt a feminine symbol, and why its meanings are so diverse that it may represent many women at once'. (Suzanne Langer: 'Philosophy in a New Key' - Dr. Langer was an advocate and follower of Ernst Cassirer's ideas).

8. (p. 12) Families of meaning are discussed in Wittgenstein;s 'Philosophical Investigations'.

9. (p. 13) Kepler's 'vis formatrix' or 'matrix formativa' was the individual soul which reacted, shaped itself and grew according to the developing geometry of the universe as represented by astrology. (The Influence of Archetypal Ideas on the Scientific Theories of

Kepler, Wolfgang Pauli, Routledge). Goethe's Ur-Pflanze, or 'original plant-form' was the universal initial ideal form which stood as pattern of development for each particular plant. It has obvious roots in Plato's 'Forms'.

Chapter II   The Logic of the Structure

1. (p. 17) 'In progressing from the idea of space to that of time, and from these two in turn to the idea of *number*, we seem to round out the world of intuition and at the same time to be referred to something beyond it. The world of tangible forms seems to recede, and in its place a new world gradually arises; a world of intellectual principles'. (Cassirer: 'Philosophy of Symbolic Forms')

2. (p. 17) Instances are - the twelve hours of the day and the twelve months of the year, divided into four seasons, each of three months. The Ionian Greeks founded twelve colonies while they themselves were divided into four tribes each of which was again split into three brotherhoods. Then there are the twelve tribes of Israel and the twelve apostles while the Book of Revelations is replete with number symbolism.

3. (p. 18) TELOS involves distance as well as ends (telephone, television, telex) while ARCHE (as in archaic, archaeology, archetype) has the meaning of origins, also, as in archbishop, the idea of authority or chief. Here it is the authority of an 'elder' over one, not the authority one seeks for oneself (TELOS) as an end. Both Arche and Telos in Greek have also the meaning of magistracy.

Chapter III   The Structure of Meaning

1. (p. 21) The difficult symbiotic link between freedom and necessity is summarized as follows: 'Freiheit ist nicht nur eingeschränkt durch Schicksal, sie schafft auch Schicksasl'. (Thomas Ring). 'Freedom is not only limited by fate, it also creates fate'. And: 'In jedem Moment schicksalhaften Geschehens Freiheit und Notwendigkeit ineinander liegen'. (Paul Tillich). 'In every moment of a fateful event freedom and necessity lie within each other'.

2. (p. 22) 'Time is the means offered to everything that will be, to be, in order not to be'.

3. (p. 23) The Meridian and Horizon are axes of meaning relating to time and space, to inner and outer, to mind and body. Karl Popper claims that animal behaviour and structure are biological analogues of theories and that theories correspond to bodily organs in their method of function. Organs and behaviour, he says, are 'tentative adaptations' to the world, as are theories, a claim implicit in astrology in which mind and body are seen as two aspects of the same.

4. (p. 24) The dualism of the Horizon diameter on the poles of which we can accommodate the identity of opposites has its counterpart in modern physics in the Principle of Complementarity whereby the electron is at once particle and wave. According to Heisenberg, 'the concept of complementarity is meant to describe a situation in which we can look at one and the same event through two different frames of reference. These two frames mutually exclude each other, but they also complement each other, and only the juxtaposition of these contradictory frames provides an exhaustive view of the appearance of the phenomena'. ("Die Teil and das Ganze"). This, in terms of physics echoes the logic of philosophy and the meaning of the Horizon in the structure of astrology. It is an indication too that one should never take one pole of meaning, e.g., the Ascendant, in isolation without considering its opposite, e.g., the Descendant, at the same time since they are two aspects of the same. We have here both the difference and the identity of opposites, the harmony in contrariety.

5. (p. 24) Bertrand Russell claimed that our bodies were just as much part of our environment as tables and chairs were. Consider, when eating, precisely when does our food cease to be part of our environment and become part of us, or, when excreting, precisely when do faeces cease to be part of us and become part of our environment. It is impossible to differentiate. We and our environment are one.

6. (p. 24) The present moment, according to Leibniz (who though German wrote in French), is 'chargé du passé et gros de l'avenir',

laden with the past and pregnant with the future. According to Whitehead 'the occasion arises as an effect facing its past and ends as a cause facing its future. In between there lies the teleology of the universe'. Whitehead says we should balance the doctrine of becoming by a doctrine of perishing - 'perishing is the initiation of becoming'. In other words the immediate past which is perishing is the mid-wife of the immediate future which is becoming, and both should be seen as factors in the present which therefore embraces more than its moment indicates. The Horizon, then, is more than a line separating past from future. It contains something of past and future within it and is astrologically more like a broad band in the horoscope than a thin line.

Professor Findlay in 'The Discipline of the Cave' writes 'no genuine event or state can incorporate *none* of the past *qua* past and none of the future *qua* future, and this is a real point made by those who confusedly object to a *knife-edge* present.' The idea that something of the future is incorporated in the present is evident in Kelly's Psychology of Personal Constructs of which the fundamental postulate is: A person's processes are psychologically channelized by the ways in which he anticipates events. (George A. Kelly: 'The Psychology of Personal Constructs, 1955, and 'A Theory of Personality, 1963, Ohio State University).

The extent of the embrace of the present is relative. The more developed the mind, the more the present will mean. An animal will react to an immediate stimulus without reflection. Its appreciation is limited to the momentary event. A human being sees the present within a personal context, embracing something of what, for him, has gone before and what is to come, of memory and anticipation. For an animal the Ascendant may be one degree; for a human being it may encompass several degrees, while for highly developed people the present may reach back into the past and forward into the future so that the Ascendant expands, so to speak, to accommodate the intellect. Similarly the Midheaven in developed people may expand in accordance with their ability to interpret sense-data supplied by the Horizon, while being restricted in the case of animals by their relatively under-developed intelligence and aesthetic appreciation. The great the intelligence and sensory range the greater the latitude permissible in interpreting 'orbs of influence' of the Meridian and Horizon. There is little point in attempting to put a figure on just how much such orbs should be enlarged as they will differ according to subject but the point that they may be enlarged is important. This point seems to have been overlooked in traditional astrology.

The Meridian and Horizon are at right-angles, i.e., at cross purposes. A prime source of misunderstanding is that we incline to judge others by their actions, but ourselves by our intentions. We can see their actions since they materialize on the Ascendant but our intentions are immaterial and invisible to others since they relate to the Midheaven and are known only to us. This is a source of serious misconception if not worse and should be borne in mind when comparing the compatibility or otherwise of two horoscopes. Somehow the Ascendant of the one must be related to the Midheaven of the other and vice-versa which means putting each into the other's shoes, a difficult, if not impossible operation for most of us since, in essence, it implies that 'thou art the other' just when each feels most alien.

7. (p. 32) The seventh house and the first represent the identity of opposites implicit in the philosophy of the Vedanta, in the Eleatics, in Plotinus and Spinoza, and most thoroughly in Hegel.

8. (p. 34) 'L'affectant et l'affecté ne font qu'un parceque la poussée du temps n'est rien d'autre que la transition d'un présent a un présent'. (Merleau-Ponty: 'La Phenomenologie de la Perception'). The stimulus and the reaction are the same since the impetus of time is nothing but the passage of one present to another'.

9. (p. 34) There are two ways of interpreting 'thou art that'. The Vedic interpretation is 'thou art Brahman', but more akin to the union of synthesis suggested by the poles of the Horizon is that of Martin Buber's duologue in his book 'I and Thou'.

10. (p. 35) J.S. Bell, a nuclear research physicist at CERN in Switzerland, published his theorem in 1964. Eight years later his findings were confirmed by the Clauser Freedman experiment at the Lawrence Berkeley Laboratory.

11. (p. 39) Each house has a 'ruler' the planet associated with the sign on its cusp and, as secondary ruler, that planet associated with the sign analogous with the house, e.g., Taurus on the third house would mean Venus as third house ruler since Venus rules Taurus, but

Mercury would be a secondary ruler since Mercury rule Gemini, the third sign. The house and sign the ruler happens to occupy becomes of some importance in interpretation.

12. (p. 39) 'Peripatetics' and 'discitur ambulando'. Aristotle used to teach while walking about (Gk. peri 'about', pateo 'to walk'. Lat. discere 'to learn', ambulando 'while walking'), a procedure typical of third house meaning.

13. (p. 42) The difference between reaction to outside stimuli (Descendant and seventh house) and instinctual reaction (Lower Heaven and fourth house) is seen in how birds react to food thrown at them compared with how they build their nests and sing. They inherit the capacity for nest-building 'in the form of a sort of chromosomal tape-recording. This instinctual knowledge is not arrived at by association of ideas, anyhow of ideas received by the animal in its own lifetime'. (P.B. Medawar: 'The Art of the Soluble'.)

14. (p. 43) The Midheaven may also be likened to the idea of 'dharma' or moral law.

Chapter IV   The Elements

1. (p. 51) 'Vier Elemente....' 'Four elements intimately related fashion life and construct the world'.

2. (p. 51) 'If you are with the Creator everything follows you - Man, Angel, Sun and Moon, Air, Fire, Earth and Stream.'

3. (p. 54) These three modes and their accompanying four elements are reflected in molecular movement and state. A molecule has three forms of energy - kinetic energy (movement in a straight line), rotational energy (spin), and vibrational energy (due to distortion). Molecular *states*, however, relate to the elements. In solids (Earth) molecules are packed tight and strongly held together. In liquids (Water) molecules slide over each other but cling to each other in motion. In gases (Air) molecules lose their clinging qualities and move freely and rapidly in all directions. If enclosed they spread and

occupy the whole enclosure. The average velocity of air molecules is over 1,000 miles an hour. In combustion (Fire) they split up into their constitutional atoms where the limit of velocity is the speed of light. There is a progression from cohesion to detachment, from slowness to rapidity, from low to high temperature. Suppose we look at the elements once again, extending the principles for which they stand as symbols:

```
FIRE    Dynamic  Energy  Function   Plasma  Chaos: Formlessness
AIR     ↓  ↑     ↓  ↑    ↓  ↑       Gases   ↓            ↑
WATER ↓  ↓       ↓  ↑    ↓  ↑       Liquids ↓            ↑
EARTH  Static    Matter  Structure  Solid   Form.  Order
```

If one applies heat to metals they melt, if to liquids the result is gases (water becomes steam), if to gases the result is a plasma in which event the atoms lose their structure and become dissassociated into electrons and ions. Heat turns the form, order and restriction of matter into the formless, freedom and expansion of energy. Structure and function, like space and time or matter and energy, form a continuum, structure being a slowed down, condensed aspect of function, function a speeded up, rarified or expanded aspect of the structure. AIR, though generally formless shows a potentiality for form in a whirlwind or tornado, WATER in a vortex or whirlpool. Only in EARTH, solid matter, does distinctive, enduring form manifest itself. The symbolism of astrology is admirably illustrative of aspects of existence whether material or not as Plato understood and set out in his *Timaeus*. In it we have a symbolic logic applicable to all aspects of the world as we know it. It will even fit the Big Bang theory of the origin of the universe. In the beginning, assuming there was one, the big explosion took place in a featureless, formlessness at an unimaginably high temperature; it is all energy. As things began to cool down they began to take shape; form and structure began to appear with gases condensing and eventually the apperance of solid matter, of which our nearest example is planet Earth.

I admit, myself, to being sceptical about the Big Bang theory and suggest it could be an illusion due to our anthropocentric viewpoint. It is difficult to see, however, how ephemaral man whose existence is but a moment in time could ever either prove or disprove it. But, since man himself in his environment expands from birth and contracts towards death, an analogy with the cosmos might turn out to be a fruitful basis for speculation. Anthropocentric again, of course, but then we can't escape that. Our view of the universe, to say nothing of science itself, is based on it. Plato's principles in the Timaeus and the symbolism of astrology are seen to operate not only throughout the world of mind and body but in the inanimate world of matter also. Aristotle, too, developed a triad of movement. In his terms there is firstly *alloiosis* or qualitative change, i.e., change from one quality to another, secondly *auxesis* and *phthisis* (increase and decrease) quantitative change or change within itself, and lastly *phora* or simple change of place, or motion. The first can be related to the Cardinal mode, the second to the Fixed mode, and the third to the Mutable mode. Again, in Indian philosophy we have the three 'Gunas', Rajas, Tamas and Sattva which can be interpreted on many levels and relate broadly to Cardinal, Fixed and Mutable respectively. In his 'Six Systems of Indian Philosophy' Professor Max Müller relates them to Hegel's thesis, antithesis and synthesis.

4. (p. 60) Ernst Kretschmer, German psychologist, ('Physique and Character', Routledge).

Chapter V Wholes, Hemispheres and Quadrants

1. (p. 63) 'The world does not hold thee, thou thyself art the world which so strongly imprisons thee.'

2. (p. 63) 'Umwelt und Innenwelt der Tiere' (Environment and Inner Environment of Animals). For those interested von Uexhüll's work is dealt with in greater detail with reference to astrology in Thomas Ring's 'Astrologische Menschenkunde'.

3. (p. 63) See also Merleau-Ponty where he states that organisms have to do with a series of environments and milieu (Umwelt, Merkwelt and Gegenwelt) in which stimuli intrude in a manner according to what they signify and are worth for the typical activity of the species under consideration. (Merleau-Ponty: 'The Phenomenology of Perception' and 'The Structure of Behaviour', Methuen).

Chapter VI   The Signs of the Zodiac

1. (p. 69) Kepler was not the first to think thus. The Pythagorean physician Alcmaeon who lived in the fifth century BC, predating Hippocrates by a generation or more had the same idea. He was a believer in 'the stars' and his ideas on health influenced medicine for centuries. To him the secret of health was harmony or balance - a balance of the physiological functions, fitting in well with the dialectic of astrology. A physician of great skill and daring he investigated the nature of sense perception, the nutrition of the embryo in the womb and the physiological changes necessary for sleep. He also did dissection and explored the Eustachian tube between ear and throat two thousand years before Bartolommeo Eustacchi re-explored it and gave his name to it. According to Burnet he was also the founder of empirical psychology. (Burnett: 'Early Greek Philosophy'). See also Prof. A.E. Taylor's critique of Plato's Timaeus, Phaedo and Phaedrus, in A.E. Taylor's 'Plato, the Man and his Work'. University Paperbacks.

2. (p. 77) 'Taurus drakontos kai taurou drakon pater', (Firmicus Maternus). 'The bull is the father of the dragon and the dragon the father of the bull'.

Chapter VII   The Geometry of Meaning

1. (p. 110) Scorpio, the sign of sex, is for its part in trine with Cancer (pregnancy and birth) and in square with Leo (creativity), joined in each case by an angle of generation. In the first case the design is inward and instinctive, in the second outward and purposive. In the first case heredity and instinct provide the motive force, in the second the libido.

Chapter VIII   Sun, Moon and Planets

1. (p. 121) Wolfgang Pauli: 'The Influence of Archetypal Ideas on Kepler's Theories', (Routledge, 1955).

2. (p. 122) See accompanying diagram.

3. (p. 128) 'Striated' muscle (Mars) is voluntary, externally motive and found in the limbs and external parts of the body. 'Smooth' muscle (Mars-Jupiter) is involuntary and relates to visceral or internal muscle. Heart muscle (Mars-Sun) is spiral, geodesic and only found in the heart itself. It will be noted that striated muscle is related to the Cardinal mode, heart muscle to the Fixed mode, and smooth muscle to the Mutable mode. Heart muscle, as befits the power centre of the body is also the hardest working contracting some 101,000 times a day or 370 million times a year without stopping. When it fails, as in coronary hear disease one should look for a difficult aspect between Sun and Mars either in the birth chart, the progressed chart or the transit chart for the day of onset. The birth chart indicates the congenital disposition, the progressed chart the increased potentiality due to the gradual development of the congenital disposition, while the transit chart relates to the circumstances prevailing on the actual day of the attack.

4. (p. 139) Planetary affinities relating to gases, liquids and solids:

Moon: Ebb and flow. Cyclic change. Reflective capacity.

Mercury: Mixture, blend, combination, compound, amalgam, alloy, catalyst, enzyme. Flexibility, variable change, oscillation.

Venus: Attraction, adhesion, cohesion, absorbtion, viscosity, osmosis, fluid exchange, sweetness, roundness, symmetry, malleability, ductility, conductivity, magnetism.

Mars: Sharpness, metallic, friction, heat, kinetic energy, repulsion, molecular speed, oxygenation, sourness, acidity, pungency.

Jupiter: Expansion, growth, warmth, overflow, effervescence, lightness, inflation, buoyancy, porosity, resilience, elasticity, cloyingness.

Saturn: Contraction, condensation, consolidation, cold, gel, frost, regularity, rigidity, hardness, weight, dullness, bitterness.

Uranus: Abnormal forms, irregularity, jaggedness, brittleness, fracture, rupture, explosiveness, fissibility, ice, lightning, electricity, spark.

Neptune: Leakage, seepage, flood, diffusion, dispersal, decay, disintegration, lubrication. Entropy.

Pluto: Destruction, transformation, transmutation, regeneration, elimination, explosiveness. Earthquake.

Neurological affinities:

Mercury:	Nerve, cell, axon. Cerebral cortex.
Venus:	Conductivity, afferent nerve impulse, sensation. Mercury-Venus = sensory nerve.
Mars:	Efferent nerve impulse. Mercury-Mars = motor nerve.
Jupiter:	Nerve tonicity.
Saturn:	Nerve inhibition, resistance.
Uranus:	Nerve reflex, synapse, spastic conditions, tics, cramps.
Neptune:	Atonicity, flaccidity, spinal fluid, paralysis. Mars-Neptune = motor paralysis, Venus-Neptune = loss of feeling, numbness, paresis, paraesthesia.

Electrical affinities:

Sun:	Power. Watts.
Moon:	Flow. Ampères.
Mercury:	Wiring, connections, electrolysis.
Venus:	Conductivity, magnetism.
Mars:	Electromotive force. Volts.
Jupiter:	Boost or surge.
Saturn:	Resistance. Ohms. Insulation.
Uranus:	Spark, contact breaker, switch, electric shock.

Chapter IX   Houses of Contention

1. (p. 145) In the accompanying chart Jupiter is the strongest planet since it rules Pisces and Sagittarius in which both Sun and Moon are placed and therefore rules them too. Moreover Jupiter is in Aquarius, the sign of intellectual discovery and in the ninth house, the house of speculative thinking. Mercury, the ruler of the Composite Ascendant, is equally strong in the tenth house conjunct Saturn while the M.C. forms a mid-point between Sun/Mercury, the Sun being the ruler of the third house, the house of innate intelligence. Uranus, the planet of discovery is in the third house and also in the intellectual sign Virgo.

Chapter X   Temporal Change

1. (p. 149) 'O admirable mathematical parentage of man. What can one say of this forest of relations and correspondences.'

2. (p. 149) The trouble with directions, sometimes called the 'radix system' is that roughly every thirty years all planets come once again into aspect with their natal counterparts. With progressions, on the other hand, only the Sun suffers from this disability. Nevertheless the radix system is often fairly accurate for periods up to 29 and beyond 31 years, or up to 59 and beyond 61 years. It is a rough and rapid method but not to be disregarded especially in respect of the outer planets.

3. (p. 151) The Thirty Degree chart propagated by the German astrologer Edith Wangemann is, in the writer's opinion, more flexible and adaptable than the better-known Forty-five Degree chart advocated by the late Reinhold Ebertin, since it enables aspects such as multiples of 15° and 7°30' to be easily recognised. In the accompanying chart oppositions across the circle indicate 15° multiple aspects and the square between Sun and Uranus is 7°30' multiple, actually 202°.12' or 7°.30' x 27. The opposition Mars - Jupiter/Pluto, i.e., 285°.52' is also a multiple aspect - 15° x 19, similarly Jupiter - Uranus/Pluto = 224°.33' = 15° x 15. Such multiple aspects are not in general astrological use but if restricted to an exactitude of one degree or less are of considerable value.

Chapter XI   Proof

1. (p. 155) 'This is the fallacy of the statistical picture: it is one sided, inasmuch as it represents only the average aspect and reality and excludes the total picture. The statistical view of the world is a mere abstraction and therefore incomplete and even fallacious...' (C.G. Jung: "Synchronicity: An Acausal Connecting Principle" (Routledge).

APPENDIX I

The five senses are accommodated in planetary symbolism as follows:

Sun: Sight. Positive function of sight, involving conscious purpose and direction - Looking, peering, examining, focusing. (Purposive)

Moon: Sight. Negative function. The eyes as receptors - seeing, registering, recording. (Unintentional)

Venus: Touch. (Unintentional)

Mars:[†] Taste. (Purposive)

Jupiter: Smell. Positive function - sniffing, scenting. (Purposive)

Saturn: Hearing. Negative function - hearing. (Unintentional)

Uranus: Hearing. Positive function - listening. (Purposive)

Neptune: Smell. Negative function - smelling, receptivity for smells. (Unitentional)

Any one of the above planets being prominent in a horoscope suggest an acuity or disturbance of the sense concerned.

Meanings of planets are emphasized in their relationships with other planets, most often when the link is between obvious opposites such as Sun and Moon, Mars and Venus, Jupiter and Saturn where the propensities of the one draw out their opposites in the other. The following is a list of some of these meanings. Once the logic of the counterpoint is understood readers will be able to complete the picture for themselves.

[†] The attribution of taste to Mars may be traditional, but in the logic of the symbolism is quite untenable. Mars indicates action, not sensation - motor-nerve force, not afferent-nerve sensation. To touch something may relate to Mars but the sensation of touch is symbolized by Venus. Similarly the activity of tasting something may relate to Mars but the sensation of taste, the taste itself, is symbolized by Venus. Venus, then, relates both to touch and taste - taste involving the tongue and palate to the Venus sign Taurus, touch concerning the skin to the Venus sign Libra.

<u>Sun</u>
Source of power
Light, heat
Radiation
Husband, father
Male hormone function
Testes
Prostate

<u>Moon</u>
Reflection of power
Reflected light, cool
Reception
Wife, mother
Female hormone function
Ovary
Womb

<u>Sun</u>
Light, heat
Radiation
Generation of life
Pungency
Husband as outgoing spouse
Father as outgoing parent

Natural authority
Magnanimous
Genial

<u>Saturn</u>
Dark, cold
Insulation, block, barrier
Extinction of life
Bitterness
Husband as restrictive spouse
Father as disciplinary, restrictive parent
Institutional authority
Mean
Serious, earnest

<u>Moon</u>
Humidity
Fluidity
Content
Volume
Plasticity
Melting
Changeability
Containing, holding
Transparency
Liquefaction
Clannishness

Imagination
Conception, reproduction
Spouse as intimate wife
Caring wife

<u>Saturn</u>
Aridity
Solidity
Form
Mass
Rigidity
Congealing, condensing
Resistance to change
Supporting
Opacity
Concretion, hardening, sclerosis
Lonesomeness, alienation, apartheid

Lack of imagination
Infertility
Spouse as aloof husband
Distant or deceased husband

<u>Venus</u>
Femininity
Softness, roundness
Sweetness
Smoothness
Viscosity
Sensation, skin
Cohesion, fusion
Union, association
Parity, equality, balance
Co-operation, peace
Receptivity
Vagina
Ingestion, lips, mouth
Venous blood flow
Construction
Anything taken in
Adjuncts of reception, tubes, apertures, passage, sheaths, valves
Harmony
Love

<u>Mars</u>
Masculinity
Sharpness, pointedness
Pungency, acidity
Roughness
Friction
Action, muscle
Splitting, disassociation
Disunion, divorce
Disparity, inequality, imbalance
Competition, opposition, war
Penetration, ejaculation
Penis
Excretion, rectum, anus
Arterial blood flow
Destruction
Anything forced out
Adjuncts of penetration, knives, swords, weapons, drills, rams
Disorder
Hate

<u>Venus</u>
Fluid balance
Ovulation
Ducts, tubes, channels for passing things through
Vagina, alimentary canal
Umbilical cord
Ingestion
Feeling
Budding
Attracting
Love of spouse, or partner
Rhythm of dance and intercourse, poetry and music

Income, movable property
Recipient of affection

<u>Moon</u>
Fluid economy
Menstruation, conception
Cells, containers, vessels for containing things
Womb, placenta, stomach
Breasts
Nutrition
Imagination, memory
Germination
Clasping, holding
Maternal love, love of family
Rhythm of tides, diurnal rhythms, monthly rhythms, menstruation
Capital, landed property
Recipient of care

<u>Venus</u>
Softness
Roundness
Association
Yielding
Conductivity

<u>Saturn</u>
Hardness
Flatness
Isolation
Unyielding
Resistance

Mars	Saturn
Sharpness	Flatness, bluntness
Cutting, stabbing	Beating
Acid, sour	Bitter
Sore	Bruised

Jupiter	Saturn
Expansion	Contraction
Increase	Decrease
Excess	Lack
Gain	Loss
Fat	Lean
Inflation	Deflation
Lightness	Heaviness
Rising	Falling
Freedom	Constriction, Determinism
Growth, hypertrophy	Atrophy
Acceleration	Deceleration
Boom	Slump
Resilience	Inelasticity
Optimism	Pessimism
Generosity	Parsimony
Speculative	Empirical
Theory	Fact
Rashness, carelessness, risk	Caution
Extolling, bombastic	Belittling
Exaggeration	Understatement
Jovial	Saturnine
Elation	Depression
Ostentatious	Unobtrusive
Spirit of justice	Letter of the Law
Liberal penal code	Draconian measures, strict discipline
Free speech	Censorship
Uninhibited manner	Inhibited, restricted, restrictive
Self overestimation	Self control, control of others
Chance	Necessity

APPENDIX II

An illustration of how the structure of astrology may be employed in elucidating meaning is eminently afforded by the tetrad of houses III, VI, IX and XII and their corresponding signs Gemini, Virgo, Sagittarius and Pisces. We have already (see p. 40) considered three aspects of this tetrad related to mythology - Zeus, Metis and the birth of Athena, and it appears, too, in the mythical foundation of Athens, disputed by Athena (Virgo) and Poseidon (Neptune, Pisces) umpired by Cecrops symbolized by Zeus, (Jupiter, Sagittarius). It was Athena who won the contest and she became the patroness of the city. As a result Greece itself came under the sign Virgo but Poseidon (Neptune), though defeated was not annihilated, merely submerged, and continued to play a large part. If one looks at a map of Greece one sees that no other country is so split in two by Earth (Virgo) and Water (Pisces). Half of Greece, the Aegean, is submerged, the territory of Poseidon, the other half is 'virgin' territory, subject to Athena. For centuries the power of Greece was maritime. Even to this day, Greece, one of the smallest countries in Europe, has one of the largest merchant fleets in the world. Mythology and actuality sometimes have a curious way of complementing each other.

To proceed from mythology to something more rational - language, an area of meaning relating to the third house and Gemini-Mercury. The third house being adjacent to the lower Meridian, the structure of language suggests something inherited, *a priori*, innate (see remarks on Chomsky, p. 39). In contrast the sixth house at right angles to it and adjacent to the Horizon (empirical, environmental) suggests not an inherited but an acquired knowledge of language. Both of these houses correspond to signs ruled by Mercury, the planet of communication.

The ninth house in opposition to the third is adjacent to the upper Meridian or Midheaven with its connotations of remote interests and long term aims, carrying with it the suggestion of a further development of language or the acquirement of foreign languages, this being entirely consonant with the meaning of its associated sign, Sagittarius and its ruler Jupiter. Moreover, here we see in operation the generative aspect of the right-angle (3rd square 6th and 6th square 5th). If we now consider the third right-angle (9th square 12th) we see that the twelfth must relate to the final consummation of language, the ineffability of mystics and the elusiveness of such enigmatically transcendant writers as the Pseudo Dionysius, again correlating perfectly with the associated mystical connotations of sign and planet - Pisces and Neptune.

If we now turn our tetrad clockwise so that the third house occupies the place of the twelfth and the twelfth that of the ninth we see that the final aim (ninth) of language must be its ineffability, its annihilation or transcendence in the silent contemplation of the mystic. Once again, too, we have an anti-clockwise progression from primitive origin to developed, final consummation, and a clockwise progression in reverse from ultimate to primitive. We have chosen one example but this geometrical progression can be applied to any house or sign in aspectual relationship with others for the further elucidation of meaning.

Further Meanings related to the Horizon and Meridian

HORIZON

Ascendant	Descendant
Proposal	Response, acceptance, refusal
Decision	Choice, equivocation
Unsociability, detachment	Sociability, attachment
Partisanship	Impartiality
Discord	Harmony, concord
Question	Answer
Lemma	Dilemma
Attack	Opposition, neutralisation
Injury to others	Injury returned
Active	Re-active
Muscular activity on environment	Sensual appreciation of environment

MERIDIAN

Midheaven	Lower Heaven
To be determined	Already determined
Conscious purpose	Unconscious motive
What I will be	What I was
The drive for the future	The thrust of the past
Future construction	Past foundation
Distance. Far from home	Proximity. Close to home
Wide open world of anticipation	Intimate world of memory

The point where the two diameters cross, the central point of the horoscope, represents Husserl's 'Natural Standpoint'. It is not the 'self' itself but the position and orientation of the self as point event (Whitehead) in space-time. Time is not, as Merleau-Ponty points out, 'a real process'. It appears as a result of the subject's relation to things. The water which will flow under the bridge tomorrow is today at its source, while the water which has just swept under the bridge is now at this moment further downstream, but from the stand-point of the said patch of water the bridge has moved upstream. Duration is relative, not 'real' and exists solely in the present, as ideal. Only the present is real for the past is no longer and the future not yet, whether we take as reference point the patch of water flowing down under the bridge or the bridge moving upstream. This does not, of course, invalidate the concept of time. It is obviously as essential as space or place to which it is inextricably bound, as space is to time, but whereas space or place appears to us outwardly as real, as the Horizon of the horoscope indicates, time or duration is felt by us inwardly as unreal, or ideal, as suggested by the Meridian. Between them time and space form a continuum for the actual appearance of events, space being apprehended by our senses, time by our intuition and reason. Like the bridge and the stream we can see time as either passing through us or alternatively ourselves as passing through time. Time, as Kant recognized, is 'interior sense', i.e., ideal, while space is exterior sense, a locus for the contemporary appearance of what we take to be real. The horoscope obligingly provides us with co-ordinates for both. In effect we hover perilously balanced between ideal and real, for without either we cannot exist. The structure of astrology eloquently emphasizes this.

As a coda to the above, since time is ideal not real some sort of immortality would appear to be a necessity since what does not exist of itself cannot perish. As Erwin Schroedinger has remarked ('Mind and Matter', Cambridge U.P.) this means a 'liberation from the tyranny of Chronos'. What we ourselves construct cannot have power over our minds. In other words he claims that present physical theory suggests the 'indestructibility of Mind by Time'.

GLOSSARY

Ascendant: The degree of the Zodiac rising on the eastern Horizon at the time of a birth or of any occurrence for which a horoscope is cast.

Aspect: An angular relationship between planets as seen from the earth, relating the qualities of one planet with another, blending them or contrasting them. The Trine (120°) and the Sextile (60°) are considered favourable or furthering. The Opposition (180°) and the Square (90°), together with the Semi-Square (45°) and the Sesqui-Square (135°) are considered difficult or hindering. The effect of the Conjunction depends on whether the planets forming it are mutually concordant or antagonistic, Sun conjunct Jupiter is concordant while Sun conjunct Saturn is antagonistic. The opposition, though a difficult aspect can, however, prove helpful through Heraclitus' 'harmony in contrariety'. In order of strength the conjunction comes first followed by opposition, trine, square, sextile and so on. There are lesser aspects such as the quintile series (see text) and the 15° multiple and 7°.30' multiple (see p. 151).

Conjunction	(☌) 0°		Opposition	(☍) 180°	
Trine	(△) 120°		Square	(□) 90°	
Sextile	(✶) 60°		Semi-Square	(∠) 45°	
Semi-Sextile	(⩗) 30°		Sesqui-Square	(⚼) 135°	
Quincunx	(⚻) 150°		Novile	(1/9) 40°	
Quintile	(Q) 72°		Bi-Quintile	(BQ) 144°	
Semi-Quintile	(SQ) 36°		Sesqui-Quintile	(SSQ) 108°	

Cusp: With regard to houses the cusp is the point of maximum effect; with regard to the Zodiac it is the dividing line between one sign and another. The cusp of the first house is the Ascendant. In western astrology the cusp of a house is usually regarded as its leading edge and this is how we have illustrated it in our charts. However, if we take into consideration the fact that the present embraces something of both past and future as Leibniz, Whitehead, Sartre, Findlay and others have demonstrated then logically the cusp of the first house, the Ascendant, should be not its leading edge but the centre of the house, similarly with the other houses. Moreover this latter view relates logically to the application and separation of aspects which also concern the future and past. The Ascendant moving to an application indicates something in the future; to exactitude, an event in the present; to a separation, something in the past. This view, (the cusp as centre of a house), is taken by Indian astrology and by a minority of western practitioners. We are inclined to support this latter view. (See accompanying chart.)

Ecliptic: The zodiacal path, eight to nine degrees wide, illustrating the Sun's apparent orbit around the Earth, as seen from the Earth. It is along this path that eclipses occur, signalled by the Moon's Nodes, Caput and Cauda Draconis.

Ephemeris: A book of tables of planetary positions for every day of each year showing the latitude and zodiacal longitude in degrees of sign.

Mundane Astrology: Astrology as it relates to world trends and the horoscopes of nations.

Orbs: The number of degrees within which an aspect is effective. There is no universal agreement on this. We have already suggested a possible range. Another, more logical since it relates to the division of the circle is as follows: Conjunction 12°, Opposition 6°, Trine 4°, Square 3°, Sextile 2°, Semi- and Sesqui-Square 1°.30', Semi-Sextile 1°, all other aspects 1°. This division was suggested by the late John Addey, former President of the Astrological Association.

Quadruplicity: Four signs divided into three groups, i.e.,
Cardinal: Aries, Cancer, Libra, Capricorn.
Fixed: Taurus, Leo, Scorpio, Aquarius.
Mutable: Gemini, Virgo, Sagittarius, Pisces.

Quintile: As aspect of 72° first proposed by Kepler - one fifth of the circle. Related aspects are 36°, the Semi-Quintile, 108°, the Sesqui-Quintile, and 144°, the Bi-Quintile.

Radix: The horoscope of a birth or of any event as contrasted with a progressed or transit horoscope.

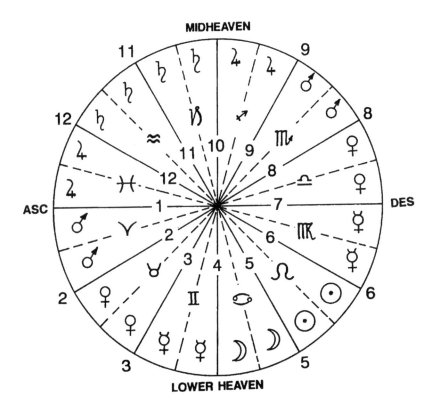

Figure 29 - Cusps as Centres of Houses
Lines indicate cusps. Interrupted lines indicate limits of houses. Here each house has two related zodiacal rulers - one suggesting external experience and the body, the other internal experience and the mind. Note that the Ascendant has Mars as its exterior or physical ruler, Jupiter as its internal or mental ruler. Similarly the Lower Heaven has the Moon as external or physical ruler, Mercury as internal or mental ruler. The Midheaven has Saturn as external or physical ruler, Jupiter as internal or mental ruler. Especially noticeable are the fifth cusp, external ruler Sun and internal ruler Moon both suggestive of the idea of creativity (fifth), and the eighth cusp, external ruler Mars and internal ruler Venus, both suggestive of the idea of sex. Such apt symbolism suggests that the cusp as the centre of a house rather than as its leading edge is a valid concept. Moreover it fits with the containment of past and future with the present.

Radix System of Directions: The Midheaven, Sun and all planets are moved forward at a mean rate of the Sun-Arc and the Moon is moved forward at its mean rate of 13°.11' per year. The Ascendant is found from the Table of Houses relating to the directed Midheaven. In Einstein's chart for the year of the General Theory the directed Asc. comes into aspect with natal Neptune (ruler of the Midheaven) & with natal Sun (on Midheaven) both within 1 degree. During the same year the directed Moon comes into aspect with Natal Jupiter/Pluto, natal Ascendant, and natal Midheaven. The symbolism of Moon - Jupiter/Pluto may be interpreted as 'explosive or metamorphous (Pluto) expansion (Jupiter) or imagination' (Moon).

Ruler: Any planet in a dominant position with regard to sign, house or chart. The ruler of a sign is that planet chiefly associated with it, e.g., Mars ruler of Aries, Jupiter of Sagittarius. Some signs have two rulers, i.e., Aquarius (Saturn & Uranus) Pisces (Jupiter & Neptune) and Aries (Mars & Pluto). The ruler of a house is primarily that planet placed within it and secondarily that planet which is the ruler of the sign occupying the cusp of the house. The ruler of the whole horoscope is a) any planet in close aspect with the Ascendant and in the first house, and b) the ruler of the Ascendant sign.

Symbols:

Planetary						
	Sun	☉		Jupiter	♃	Im-personal
	Moon	☽	Personal	Saturn	♄	
	Mercury	☿		Uranus	♅	
	Venus	♀	Inter-Personal	Neptune	♆	Para-personal
	Mars	♂		Pluto	♇	

Zodiacal	Aries ♈	Leo ♌	Sagittarius ♐	FIRE
	Taurus ♉	Virgo ♍	Capricorn ♑	EARTH
	Gemini ♊	Libra ♎	Aquarius ♒	AIR
	Cancer ♋	Scorpio ♏	Pisces ♓	WATER

Transit: The passage of a planet over the natal Meridian, Horizon or natal position of Sun, Moon or any planet. Transits may also be significant by aspect with natal positions. They are obtained from the ephemeris of the year in question.

Triplicities: The three groups (Cardinal, Fixed and Mutable) of the four elements (Fire, Air, Water, Earth).

BIBLIOGRAPHY

Addey, John. 'Harmonics in Astrology'. (Urania Trust, 2nd edition 1996).

Baigent, M, Campion, N. and Harvey, C. 'Mundane Astrology'. (Aquarian Press, 1984).

Barfield, Owen. 'Saving the Appearances'. (Faber, 1957).

Bateson, Gregory. 'Mind and Nature, a Necessary Unity'. (Fontana, 1980).

Blair, Lawrence. 'Rhythms of Vision'. (Paladin, 1976).

Buber, Martin. 'I and Thou'. (Scribners New York, 1958).

Butler, Christopher. 'Number Symbolism'. (Routledge).

Campion, N. 'The Book of World Horoscopes'. (Aquarius Press, 1988).

Cassirer, Ernst. 'The Philosophy of Symbolic Forms'. (Yale, 1955).

Critchlow, Keith. 'Order in Space. (Thames & Hudson, 1969). 'Time Stands Still'. (Gordon Fraser, 1979).

Dean, G., Ed. 'Recent Advances in Natal Astrology'. (Astrological Association, 1977).

Ebertin, Reinhold. 'The Combination of Stellar Influences'. (Ebertin Verlag, Aalen, Württemberg, 1940). 'Anatomische Entsprechungen der Tierkreisgrade'.

Eliade, Mircea. 'The Myth of the Eternal Return'. (Routledge, 1955). 'The Two and the One'. (Harvil Press, 1965).

Elwell, D. 'Cosmic Loom'. (Unwin Hyman).

Ferrière, Adolphe. 'Psychological Types'. (Heinemann, 1958).

Findlay, J.N. 'The Discipline of the Cave'. (Unwin, 1966). 'The Transcendence of the Cave'. (Unwin, 1967).

Franz, Marie Louise von. 'Number and Time'. (Rider, 1974).

Freeman, K. 'Companion to the Pre-Socratic Philosophers'. (Blackwell, 1949).

Gamow, G. 'One, Two, Three..... Infinity'. (Viking, N.Y., 1947).

Gauquelin, M. 'L'Influence des Astres'. (Paris, 1955).
'Les Hommes et les Astres'. (Paris, 1960).

Ghyka, Matila. 'Geometrical Composition and Design'. (Tiranti, 1956).

Green, Liz. 'Relating'. (Coventure, London, 1977).
'Saturn'. (Weiser, New York).

Grene, Marjorie, Ed. 'Anatomy of Knowledge'. (Routledge, 1969).

Harding, M. and Harvey, C. 'Working with Astrology'. (Arkana, 1990).

Harding, M. 'Hymns to the Ancient Gods'. (Arkana, 1992).

Harvey, Ronald. 'Our Fragmented World'. (Green Books, 1988).

Hegel, G.W.F. See W.T. Stace. 'The Philosophy of Hegel'. (Dover, N.Y., 1955).

Heisenberg, W. 'Physics and Philosophy'. (Allen & Unwin, 1963).

Heitler, W. 'Man and Science'. (Oliver & Boyd, 1963).

Helm, E.E. 'The Vibrating String of the Pythagoreans'. (Article in Scientific American, Dec. 1967).

Huntley, H.E. 'The Divine Proportion'. (Dover, New York, 1970).

Huxley, Aldous. 'The Perennial Philosophy'. (Chatto & Windus, 1947).
'Ends and Means'. (Chatto & Windus, 1938).

Jaspers, Karl. 'The Great Philosophers'. (Rupert Hart Davis).

Jones, Roger. 'Physics as Metaphor'. (Abacus, 1983).

Jung, Carl. 'Psychological Types'. (Routledge, 1959).
'Synchronicity: An Acausal Connecting Principle'. (Routledge, 1955).

Kant, Immanuel. 'The Critique of Pure Reason'.

Keyserling, Hermann. 'Das Weltbild der Astrologie'.

Klibansky, Saxl & Panovsky. 'Saturn and Melancholy'. (Nelson, 1964).

Klöckler, H. Freiherr von. 'Grundlagen für die Astrologische Deutung'. (Berlin, 1952).
'Astrologie als Erfahrungswissenschaft'. (Leipzig, 1927).

Koch, W.A. 'Aspektlehre nach Johannes Kepler'. (Hamburg, 1952).
'Innenmensch und Assenmensch'. (Zenit Verlag, München, 1956).

Land, Frank. 'The Language of Mathematics'. (Murray, 1960).

Langer, Suzanne. 'Philosophy in a New Key'. (Harvard, 1942).

Lehrs, Ernst. 'Man of Matter'. (Faber, 1958).

Merleau-Ponty, M. 'The Phenomenology of Perception'.

Medawar, P. 'The Art of the Soluble'.

Murti, T.R.V. 'The Central Philosophy of Buddhism'. (Unwin, 1980).

Nicholas of Cusa. 'Of Learned Ignorance'. (Routledge).

Nicoll, Maurice. 'Living Time'. (Vincent Stuart, 1952).

Ogden, C.K. 'Opposition: A Linguistic and Psychological Analysis'. (Kegan Paul, 1932).

Pauli, Wolfgang. 'The Influence of Archetypal Ideas on Kepler's Theories'. (Routledge, 1955).

Plotinus. 'The Second Ennead. On Whether the Stars are Causes'.

Polanyi, Michael. 'The Tacit Dimension'. (Routledge).
'Personal Knowledge'. (Routledge, 1958).

Popper, Sir Karl. 'The Logic of Scientific Discovery'. (Hutchinson, 1959).
'Conjectures and Refutations'. (London, 1962).

Prigogine, I. & Stengers, I. 'Order out of Chaos'. (Flamingo, 1984).

Pyllkänen, Paavo. 'The Search for Meaning'. (Crucible, 1989).

Ribot, T. 'Essay on the Creative Imagination'. (Kegan Paul, 1906).

Ring, Thomas. 'Astrologische Menschenkunde'. (Rascher Verlag, Zurich, 1959). 'Tierkreis und Menschlicher Organismus'. (Ebertin Verlag).

Rudhyar, Dane. 'The Astrology of Personality'. (Servire, The Hague, 1963).

Russell, Bertrand. 'The Problems of Philosophy'. (Oxford U.P., 1967).
'A History of Western Philosophy'. (Allen & Unwin, 1948).
'Human Knowledge. Its Scope and Limits'. (Allen & Unwin, 1948).

Sartre, Jean-Paul. 'Being and Nothingness'. (Methuen).
'Existentialism is a Humanism'.
'The Emotions: Outline of a Theory'. (Philosophical Library, 1948).

Scheler, Max. 'The Nature of Sympathy'. (Routledge, 1954).

Schmidt, Thomas. 'Musik und Kosmos als Schöpfungswunder'. (Frankfurt, 1974).

Schneer, C.J. 'The Search for Order'. (E.U.P., 1960).

Schroedinger, Erwin. 'What is Life'. (Cambridge U.P., 1967)
'Mind and Matter'. (Cambridge U.P., 1967).

Schumacher, E.F. 'A Guide for the Perplexed'. (Abacus, 1978).

Shallis, M. 'On Time'. (Pelican, 1983).

Sheldon, William. 'The Varieties of Temperament'. (Harper & Row, N.Y.).

Stace, W.T. 'The Philosophy of Hegel'. (Dover, N.Y., 1955).

Talbot, Michael. 'Mysticism and the New Physics'. (Routledge, 1981).

Taylor, A.E. 'Elements of Metaphysics'. (Methuen, 1961).
'Plato, the Man and his Work'. (Methuen, 1966).

Thompson, D'Arcy Wentworth. 'On Growth and Form'. (Cambridge U.P., 1963).

Uexküll, Jakob von. 'Umwelt und Innenwelt der Tiere'. (Berlin, 1921).
'Theoretische Biologie'. (Berlin, 1938).

Valens, E.G. 'The Number of Things'. (Methuen).

Valéry, Paul. 'Regards sur le Monde Actuel'. (Gallimard, Paris, 1945).

Volguine, A. 'La Technique des Revolutions Solaires'. (Cahiers Astrologiques, Nice, 1937).

Waddington, C.H. 'Towards a Theoretical Biology'. (Edin. U.P., 1970).

Whitehead, A.N. 'Science and the Modern World'. (Cambridge, 1925).
'Process and Reality'. (Cambridge, 1929).
'Adventures of Ideas'. (Cambridge, 1933).
'The Concept of Nature'. (Cambridge, 1920).

Whiteman, M. 'The Philosophy of Space and Time'. (Allen & Unwin, 1967).

Whyte, L.L. 'Accent on Form'. (Routledge, 1955).
'Aspects of Form'. (Lund Humphries, 1968).

Woodger, J.A. 'The Biological Principles'. (Routledge, 1967).

Yates, Frances. 'Giordano Bruno and the Hermetic Tradition'. (Routledge, 1964).

INDEX

Accusative case 40, 110
actuality 15, 16
Addey, John 157, 188
Aenesidemus 5
affinity 6, 7, 11, 107
Alcmaeon of Croton 69, 107, 176
altruism 24, 159
analogy 6, 7, 139
Angelus Silesius 7, 51, 63
anima, animus 122
anticipation 24, 111
antithesis 26, 35, 107, 110, 175
Aquarius 46, 89, 105
Aquinas, Thomas 12
Arbitrium 18, 24
Arche 18, 22, 39, 43, 169
Aries 25, 31, 70, 74, 100, 111, 136
Aristophanes 159
Aristotle 12, 13, 15, 17, 39, 41, 52, 107, 111, 173, 175
Ascendant 24, 25, 31, 98, 159, 171, 172, 185, 187
Ascendant (Derived) 145
Ascendant (Composite) 146
Ascendant, location of 98
aspects 27, 110, 111, 116, 117, 187, 188
Athena Parthenos 40, 184
Atropos 21
Augustine of Hippo 44
authority 42, 43, 44, 47, 85

Balance 32, 71, 73, 118, 146
Becoming, Being 6, 22, 25, 161
Bell's Theorem 35, 36, 172
Bender, Hans 3
Bergson, Henri 14
Bernard, Claude 165
body 24, 98
body, parts of 99
Bohr, Niels 4, 158
Bonatti, Guido 118
Book of Changes 17
Buber, Martin 172

Cancer 83, 99, 103
Capricorn 84, 99, 103
Caput Draconis 138
Cardinal signs 53, 58, 59, 175, 188
Cassirer, Ernst 3, 4, 17, 50, 147, 168
categories 6, 8, 10, 11, 17, 25
causality 13, 18
centrifugal, centripetal 124, 125
cerebrotonia 59, 60
Chomsky, Noam 39
Claudel, Paul 22
coincident birthdates 156, 157
complementarity 122, 170
coniunctio oppositorum 34, 40, 122, 160
conjunction 118
constellations 69
convention 4, 5
convergent thinking 156
Copernicus 4, 5, 7, 167
cosmos 94, 112, 115, 165
Crick, Francis 153
cusps 187, 189
cyclothyme 60, 61

Deduction of meaning 11, 82, 83, 116
Derrida 39
Descendant 18, 23, 24, 32, 159, 170, 173, 185
design 13, 14
dialectic 10, 35, 36
directions 149, 152, 179, 190
divergent thinking 156
divine proportion 112, 115
dodecahedron 109, 111, 112, 115
D N A 17, 153
Driesch, Hans 3, 14

Ebertin, Reinhold 119, 179
Eddington, Sir Arthur 112, 153
egalitarianism 14, 20
ego 24, 31, 159
Einstein 4, 7, 47, 96, 133, 141, 142, 146, 151, 152, 153, 154, 158, 190
Elements 51, 52, 53, 54, 55, 56, 57, 58, 59, 60, 61, 62, 173, 174
Eliade, Mercia 121
Empedocles 33, 51
enantiodromia 34
entelechy 12, 13, 14, 15, 18
environment 24

Equal House system 144, 145, 146, 147
equality 20, 24, 122
ethics 20, 162, 163
Eureka experience 132, 139, 161
extroversion 53, 58
Eysenck, Hans 155

Facultas formatrix 13
family 11, 12, 42
father 42, 43, 44, 125, 130
Fechner's Law 113, 118
Fibonacci Series 113, 114, 117
Findlay, J.N. 171
Firebrace, Brigadier 146
fixed signs 53, 54, 55, 56, 58, 59
Franz, Marie Louise von 17
free-will 18, 21, 23, 24, 110
Freud 44
future 21, 22, 24, 43

Galen 13
Galileo 7, 111
Gauquelin, Michel 41, 50, 155
Gemini 79, 82, 99, 102
genetic code 17
genitive case 40, 110
geometry of meaning 107
Gestalt 8, 107, 155, 168
Goethe 12, 13, 14, 132, 169
Golden Section 112, 113, 117, 118
Gunas 53, 175

Harmony 26, 34, 72, 160
Harvey, William 5
Hegel 9, 10, 12, 13, 14, 26, 34, 35, 36, 160, 161, 164, 172, 175
Heisenberg, Werner 112, 131, 158, 170
hemispheres 63
Heraclitus 26, 34, 72
heredity 22, 40, 44, 45
heuristic instrument 8
hierarchy 15, 20, 22, 163
higher octave planets 137
Hippocrates 11
Hitler 118
Horizon 3, 4, 6, 17, 18, 19, 20, 21, 22, 23, 24, 25, 65, 170, 171, 172, 185
horoscope 8, 10
houses 26-50, 141

humours 51
Husserl, Edmund 10, 12, 186
Huxley, Aldous 162, 163

Ideal 6, 10
Ideas, The 8, 9, 10, 11
introversion 53, 58
intuition 139

Jaspers, Karl 15, 168
Jung, Carl 10, 17, 23, 29, 34, 62, 122, 130, 179
Jupiter 129

Kant 9, 17, 18, 107, 112, 156, 160, 161, 186
Kennedy, John 66
Kepler 7, 13, 69, 98, 107, 111, 112, 117, 160, 168, 176, 188
Klöckler, Freiherr von 3
Kretschmer 51, 60

Lachesis 21
Langer, Suzanne 168
language 4, 21
Leibniz 170, 187
Leo 87, 99, 104
libido 110
Libra 71, 99, 100
limbo 156, 168
logarithmic rhythm 113
logarithmic spiral 113
Lower Heaven 18, 21, 22, 23

Mars 127, 128
Marx, Karl 14, 46, 91
Maternus, Firmicus 176
mathematics 115
Medawar, P.B. 173
megiston methema 8, 161, 162, 168
memory 22, 23, 24, 42
Mercury 82, 126
Meridian 3, 4, 6, 17, 18, 19, 21, 22, 23, 25, 162, 163, 170, 185
Merleau-Ponty, M. 172, 175, 186
methexis 8, 10, 11, 157
Midheaven 22, 25
modes 53, 54, 55, 56, 58, 59, 188
Moon 15, 124, 168
Morinus 145
mother 12, 42, 43, 124

Mozart 118
molecular states 173
mutable signs 54, 55, 56, 58, 59, 175, 177, 188
muscle 177

Naibod, Valentin 149
necessity 21, 22, 110
neo-Platonist 12
Neptune 6, 134, 135, 136, 137
Newton 7
nominative case 40, 110
noumenon 9, 156
number 17, 112, 169

objectivity 24
octave, higher 137
opposition 29, 30, 107, 110
opposites, extrinsic 122, 123
opposites, intrinsic 122, 123
orbs 118, 152, 188

Palladio, Andrea 113
Pauli, Wolfgang 121, 158, 169
parents 22, 42, 44, 113
Parthenon 22, 42, 44, 113
participation 7
particulars 6, 10, 11, 12, 16, 52
past 21, 22
Pasteur 3
pentagon, pentagram 110, 111, 112, 117, 118
Perennial Philosophy 163
peripatetics 39, 173
phenomenon 8, 9, 10, 11
Phidias 113
Picasso 61
Pico della Mirandola 12
Pisces 94, 99, 106
Planck, Max 4, 133, 155
planetary affinities 177
planetary emphasis 61
Plato   7-12, 15, 21, 39, 52, 109-112, 115, 147, 157, 160, 161, 164, 168, 174-176
Platonic Solids 109, 111, 115, 116, 164
Plotinus 142, 164, 172
Pluto 6, 136, 137, 138
Popper, Karl 5, 47, 155, 156, 170
Porphyry 142, 143
potential 6, 8, 9, 10, 12, 13, 15, 16, 19, 23

predisposition ... 6
prejudice ... 157
present ... 21, 24, 25, 170, 171, 172, 186, 187
progressions ... 149, 179
projection ... 34, 35
proof ... 155
Protagoras ... 4
Ptolemy ... 144, 202
Pythagoreans ... 4, 17, 69, 107, 109, 118, 167, 176

Quadrants ... 63
quadrivium ... 17
quadruplicities ... 53, 54, 56, 58, 188
qualities ... 52, 53, 56
quantum theory ... 4, 5, 10, 36, 112, 131, 133, 135, 156, 168
Quinta Essentia ... 109, 118
quintile aspects ... 111, 117, 118

Reality ... 6
Receptacle, Plato's ... 12
reductionism ... 155, 156
reincarnation ... 111
relativity, theory of ... 4, 150, 151
Renaissance ... 4, 7, 12, 113
Republic, Plato's ... 21, 111
Ribot ... 7, 139
Ring, Thomas ... 3, 167, 169, 175
RNA ... 17
royal family ... 156
Rudhyar, Dane ... 3
ruler ... 172, 190
Russell, Bertrand ... 161, 168, 170

Sagittarius ... 80, 82, 99, 102
Sartre, Jean-Paul ... 31
Saturn ... 6, 11, 129, 130
Schiller ... 51
schizothyme ... 60
Schopenhauer ... 17
Schroedinger, Erwin ... 112, 156, 186
Schumacher, F. ... 165
science ... 4, 5
Scorpio ... 76, 99, 101
Sheldon, William ... 59
signs, zodiacal ... 69-106
Socrates ... 15, 160
solar return ... 150, 151, 153

somatotonia	59, 60
space-time	11, 16, 17, 18, 23
Spengler, Oswald	14
Speusippus	109
Spindle of Necessity	21, 22, 110
Spira Mirabilis	113, 114, 115, 164
square aspect	107, 110, 187
Stace, W.T.	35
statistics	156, 179
structure	17, 18, 19, 21, 22, 23, 24, 25, 26, 27, 28, 29
studium generale	17
subjectivity	24, 31
Sun	125
Sun-arc	149, 152
syllogism	17, 107
symbols	3, 4, 5, 6, 7, 8, 9, 10, 11, 12, 13, 14, 15
sympathy of all things	11
Symposium, Plato's	15
synthesis	34, 35
Tao, the	163
Taurus	25, 75, 99, 101
teleology	12, 13, 14, 18
Telos	18, 22, 169
temperament	51, 59, 60
thesis	26, 33, 35, 107, 110
thirty degree chart	151, 179
Thompson, D'Arcy	115
Tillich, Paul	121, 169
time	18, 22, 170, 186
Toynbee, Arnold	14
transits	149
trans-Saturnian planets	6, 140
trine aspect	107, 110, 187
triplicities	53, 54, 55, 57
trivium	17
Uexküll, Jakob von	63, 175
universals	6, 10, 11, 12, 15, 16, 25, 52, 58
Unus Mundus	10
Uranus	6, 131, 132, 133
Valery, Paul	149, 162
Vedas	34
Venus	126, 127
Vico, Giambattista	14
Virgo	92, 99, 105

Viscerotonia 59, 60

Waddington 13
Watson, James 153, 154
Wells, H.G. 156
Whitehead, Alfred North 9, 12, 23, 41, 145, 168, 171, 186
Whiteman, Michael 10
wholes 63, 64, 65, 66, 67
Woodger 13
Wundt 51

Yang and Yin 122

Zen 9, 164
zodiacal signs 69-106
Zola, Emile 23